VIRTUOSO

HARVEY SACHS

ᴠIRTUOSO

The Life and Art of

NICCOLÒ PAGANINI · FRANZ LISZT

ANTON RUBINSTEIN

IGNACE JAN PADEREWSKI

FRITZ KREISLER

PABLO CASALS · WANDA LANDOWSKA

VLADIMIR HOROWITZ

GLENN GOULD

with 45 illustrations

THAMES AND HUDSON

To Barbara

© 1982 Harvey Sachs

First published in the USA in 1982 by Thames and Hudson Inc.,
500 Fifth Avenue, New York, New York 10110

Library of Congress Catalog Card Number 82-80491

Printed and bound in Great Britain

Contents

✤✤

Acknowledgments

I wish to express particular thanks to Profs. Greta Kraus and Robert Finch of the University of Toronto, to Miss Denise Restout of Lakeville, Connecticut, and to my wife, Barbara, for their assistance in the chapter on Landowska. Miss Giulia Forni of Milan, Miss Judith Silver of London and Mr Philip Wults of Toronto contributed useful information on Rubinstein. My thanks also go to the staffs of the British Institute of Recorded Sound, London, and the Museum of Broadcasting, New York, for their cooperation, and to that of Thames and Hudson for their work on this book's behalf.

H.S.

For permission to quote from various books I am grateful to the following publishers and authors: *Conversations with Casals* by J. M. Corredor (trans. by A. Mangeot). London: Hutchinson (Hutchinson Publishing Group Ltd) 1956. *Paganini the Genoese* by G. I. C. de Courcy. Norman: University of Oklahoma Press 1957. *Joys and Sorrows* by Pablo Casals as told to Albert E. Kahn. New York: Simon & Schuster 1970. *Glenn Gould: Music and Mind* by Geoffrey Payzant, copyright 1978 by Van Nostrand Reinhold Publishers, Toronto, Canada.

Plate numbers are in roman type and page numbers of in-text illustrations in italic.
American Heritage 31; Bayonne, Musée Bonnat, Photo Giraudon 2; The Bettmann Archive Inc. 32, *151*; Budapest, Magyar Nemzeti Múzeum 7; CBS Records, New York 21, 30, 33, 35, 36, *197*; CBS Records, London 34; Culver Pictures 18, 29; The Granger Collection 20; © Karsh, Ottawa 22; The Landowska Center 23, 24, 25, 26, 27, 28, *152*; By courtesy of the National Portrait Gallery, London 3, 4; City of Manchester Art Galleries, Photo courtesy of the Courtauld Institute of Art 1; Photo courtesy RCA Records 17, 19; Steinway & Sons, New York 11; United Press International Photo 13, 14, 16; Wide World Photo 15.

Introduction

❖❖❖❖❖❖❖❖❖❖❖❖❖❖❖❖❖❖❖❖❖❖❖❖❖❖❖❖❖❖❖❖❖❖❖❖❖❖

A certain pianist . . . hired women for twenty francs a concert to simulate fainting in the midst of his playing of a fantasia attacked so fast that it would have been humanly impossible to carry on at that speed to the end. Once, in Paris, the hired woman, having fallen soundly asleep, missed her cue; the pianist was playing Weber's Concerto. Counting on the fainting of this woman to interrupt the finale, he had started it at an impossible tempo. What to do? Flounder like a vulgar pianist or simulate a lapse of memory? No, he simply played the rôle of the hired woman and fainted himself. The audience rushed to the help of the pianist, who was all the more phenomenal, since he added to his lightning performance a fragile and sensitive nature. He was carried backstage; men applauded frantically, women waved their handkerchiefs, and the fainting woman, waking up, really fainted, perhaps in despair at having missed her cue.

Wanda Landowska, in *Landowska on Music*[1]

IN THE WORLD OF MUSIC, 'virtuoso' has come to refer to an instrumentalist of exceptional ability, particularly as regards technical prowess. It is often a word used with contempt, especially by composers. One may recall, for example, Ernest Bloch's statement about the 'repugnant obsequiousness of virtuosi who seek to flatter the public'. Many of the world's foremost virtuosi are commonly believed to occupy an artistic rank somewhere between that of the escape artist and that of the trained seal. This notion is not entirely without foundation; yet there are many performers who merit much higher consideration.

In 1882 Anton Rubinstein, then in his fifties and at the peak of his fame, invited violinist Eugène Ysaÿe, twenty-four and just beginning to build a career for himself, to participate with him in a short concert tour of Norway. Their performances were received with great enthusiasm. At the end of the series Rubinstein sent his young colleague a letter which demonstrates a painfully keen awareness of the musical interpreter's philosophical dilemma:

Do not allow yourself to be carried away by the outward signs of success. You may think at times that you have given yourself entirely to a work and its composer; but the audience may not have felt anything of what you thought you were expressing. There is invariably a conflict between your conception of a work and that of your audience. Always keep before you your one main objective, which must be to express the music according to your understanding and feelings, and not merely to give pleasure to those who listen. You have reached the point where it is within your power to give pleasure; what you have to do now is . . . to drink your fill of the bitter wine of triumph.[2]

Rubinstein's letter indicates that there are performing musicians who are concerned with ideas considerably deeper than those we commonly read about in the music journals' 'exclusive' interviews. Some artists occasionally take the time to consider what it is they do to their public, to the music they play and to themselves every time they walk on stage.

From a purely musical point of view, for instance, it will amaze some people to learn that Paganini, who would have taught himself to play the violin with his feet, had that been necessary to impress his public, got the greatest musical satisfaction from endlessly studying and participating in private readings of the Beethoven string quartets, those most intimate and intellectually demanding of works. Liszt, another archetypal virtuoso, tired of and gave up his performing career to devote himself to composition. And many of the others whose careers will be examined in this book had nothing but contempt for the virtuoso in his unalloyed, acrobatic form. Clearly artists like Kreisler, Casals and Landowska were aware that the vast majority of performances of music have a great deal more to do with performance than with music. What made them unusual was their primary concern with conveying the musical image as they perceived it rather than dazzling an audience at whatever cost to the material at hand.

But the virtuoso question is not so easily resolved. Paderewski realized at the outset of his career that his effect on the public was achieved more through his personality than through any real pianistic ability – a singularly honest and illuminating admission. The nature of the performing arts is such that most successful performers are endowed with great drive and self-confidence – characteristics which in themselves seem to fascinate large segments of the public. And here the matter becomes still more complicated. Setting aside the problem of technical accomplishment, it is obvious that the music of Bach, Mozart and Beethoven cannot be adequately served by interpreters lacking in intelligence, conviction and sensitivity. All too often one hears pieces played 'correctly' by mindless, spineless and colourless musicians who ought to be kept as far as possible from the performing arena. On the other hand, excesses or abuses of intelligence, conviction and sensitivity have been known to get in the way of performers and to lead them to mannerism and even megalomania. Stravinsky's statement that great conductors, like great actors, can only play themselves is necessarily true of all outstanding performers; but one must not forget that it is just as true of mediocre and bad performers. No one, however dedicated, can translate himself into the person who created the work being interpreted. For that matter, the creator himself, as interpreter of his own work, never sees it in exactly the same light from one performance to the next.

One may then determine that the question is a moral one – that seeking to understand and to reproduce a work's essence is the task of truly great musicians, and that those who look at a musical score as a complicated game that can be played in any number of interesting ways are somehow delinquent. I sympathize with this philosophy of artistic morality; and most of the performances I remember with the greatest pleasure, most of the recordings I listen to with the greatest frequency, are the work of artists who feel or felt the weight of that particular kind of responsibility. Yet I admit that from time to time I have been enlightened and even moved by performances, or by parts of performances, by artists who do not seem to feel such constraints.

It would seem fair to observe that a great performance is one whose internal logic matches and complements that of the work being performed. But who is to determine, who shall define, the elements of a musical structure? Who is to say how Mozart, in *The Magic Flute*, wanted us to regard his oddly jaunty setting of the words 'Tod und Verzweiflung war sein Lohn' ('Death and despair were his reward'), or precisely what Brahms meant by writing the ambiguous words *Un poco sostenuto* (somewhat sustained) as the tempo indication for the introduction to the first movement of his First Symphony? Do the slur marks over the left hand in the third of Chopin's Preludes prescribe a truly *legato* articulation, or do they merely indicate the sweep of the phrasing? These are crucial questions to the performer; and there are no incontestable answers to them or to the hundreds of thousands of similar problems – the parts whose sum makes the whole.

9

What happens in the end is that those of us who take our music seriously say, in effect, to a performer – each of us in his own egocentric way – 'If you can convince me, move me, according to my criteria, you are right; if you cannot, you are wrong.' Some will tell us that this is incorrect, that in fact there are national–historical performance traditions which have a graven, immutable and unarguable validity. While it is true to say that musicians living in certain places at certain times assimilate, broadly speaking, the indigenous and current musical language, one need only compare a Beethoven symphony as conducted by Weingartner with the same work as conducted by Furtwängler, or a Verdi aria as sung by Gigli and by Martinelli, or a Chopin nocturne as played by Paderewski and by Hofmann, to realize the folly of carrying the implications of this facile notion too far. Two very great heirs to two very old musical traditions have given us their frank opinions on the subject. Mahler said, 'Tradition is slovenliness'; and Toscanini, his contemporary, said, 'Today's tradition is yesterday's bad performance'.

If writing about composers is the work of cultural middlemen, writing about performers is the work of middlemen's middlemen. Yet as I began my preparatory research for this book, the old 'music performance' paradox or oxymoron began to annoy me again, as it has annoyed me in the past. 'Music': an intimate, subtle, highly complex form of expression; 'performance': an extrovert, shameless, gladiatorial means of expression. The conflict is an eternal one and the ways of resolving it are so numerous and varied that they defy definition; and therein, for me, lies the interest of this type of study.

All of the following chapters contain, in one form or another, biographical information on their protagonists. This is essential if the reader is to orientate himself. But the book is not fundamentally biographical; and although I have mentioned, for example, that Liszt is said to have been to bed with Marie Duplessis and Lola Montez (not simultaneously), I have not dwelt on that aspect of his life. Those two ladies appear to have entertained in a similar way quite a few other gentlemen – none of whom, however, was as renowned a pianist as Liszt. Likewise, we do not remember Paganini because he ran a gambling casino, Casals because he enjoyed playing tennis or Landowska because she liked scatological humour. I hope that this book is enjoyable; but I have assumed that the main reason for reading it is to learn what it was that made these performers extraordinary.

Each career investigated here comprises within itself many attitudes towards the instrumentalist's craft. These lives were selected because together they make up an interesting and diverse group. They are by no means being proposed as the nine 'greatest' virtuosi. An attempt at such a selection would be both ridiculous and fruitless.

We began with Paganini and Liszt, on whom the entire modern concept of the virtuoso and virtuosity is based. Before the nineteenth century there were, of course, superb and renowned instrumentalists. But to musicians of the late Renaissance and successive periods the ideal performer was the one who most successfully achieved an attitude of *sprezzatura* (literally 'contempt', but better rendered as 'nonchalance') by giving the appearance of playing even the most difficult passages with the greatest ease, and of not caring about the effect his playing made upon an audience. A twentieth-century equivalent of this attitude was put forward by Richard Strauss when, in inveighing against the excessively graphic gestures of some conductors, he said that a good conductor does not perspire: he makes the audience perspire. But nearly two centuries earlier some musicians were beginning to react against excesses in the other direction. Carl Philipp Emanuel Bach, in his famous *Essay on the True Art of Playing Keyboard Instruments* (1759), warned that

a musician cannot move others unless he too is moved. . . . In languishing, sad passages, the performer must languish and grow sad. Thus will the expression of the piece be more clearly perceived by the audience. . . . Similarly, in lively, joyous passages, the executant must again put himself into the appropriate mood. And so, constantly varying the passions, he will barely quiet one before he rouses another. . . . Those who maintain that all of this can be accomplished without gesture will retract their words when, owing to their insensibility, they find themselves obliged to sit like a statue before their instrument. . . . Fitting expressions help the listener to understand our meaning. . . .[3]

C. P. E. Bach was considered by his immediate successors to have been the forerunner of the Romantic movement in music. The poet Klopstock said of him that he 'united novelty and beauty' and 'raised the art of performance through teaching and practice to its perfection'.[4] Haydn, Mozart and Beethoven, whom E. T. A. Hoffman and other contemporaries considered to be the first great Romantic composers, all had the greatest respect for

C. P. E. Bach's compositions and for the book cited above. (Beethoven even had his students procure the book and use it as a supplementary text for their lessons.) With the changes in compositional styles came changes in performing styles; but little did C. P. E. Bach know that in encouraging more expressive playing, he was helping to prepare the way for a breed of performers whom he would have considered monstrosities.

The 'performer's mentality' has probably existed in certain individuals since the dawn of the human species; but Paganini and Liszt are worthy of special study because they created the notion of the instrumentalist as hero, genius and superman, while at the same time personifying that notion and fulfilling it in a way that no once since has ever achieved. 'Just as well!' some might legitimately add. Yet every performing musician since these two men conquered Europe 150 years ago has inherited, consciously or unconsciously, a legend and a point of view which he has had to confront and deal with in one way or another. One could as easily consider writing a history of physics without mentioning Newton as writing a book on virtuosi without including Paganini and Liszt.

Anton Rubinstein was, after Liszt, the most celebrated pianist of the nineteenth century. He was also a man of tremendous energy and intelligence, whose name has nearly been forgotten because his compositions have not been successful in the long term and because he did not have a flamboyant enough personality to attract journalistic legend-makers. Yet the flowering of Russian musical life from Tchaikovsky's day onwards owes a great deal to Rubinstein, as does the reform of the international concert repertoire. His marathon tour of the United States in 1872–3 was the first one undertaken there by a major European virtuoso. For all these reasons, I have devoted more attention to this extraordinary but generally overlooked musician than to anyone else in this book.

Ignace Jan Paderewski was one of the very few performing musicians who were transformed into mythical figures in their own day. Although he began his career as a professional pianist rather late, his playing and his grand manner brought him great success throughout the world. When the Polish nation was re-established after the First World War, he became its prime minister – the culmination of a life-long devotion to his country's destiny. His is one of the most remarkable of all the virtuosi's lives.

Although he began his performing career at the age of ten, Fritz Kreisler abandoned it a few years later in order to study medicine; then, after several years in the Austrian army, he returned to active concert life. Kreisler was a polyglot and a man of wide culture; he was loved as well as respected by the majority of his colleagues; and the expressiveness of his sound exerted a great influence on later generations of violinists.

Pablo Casals revolutionized cello technique, fixed the cello's reputation as a virtuoso instrument and, like Kreisler, established through his playing a point of reference for several generations of instrumentalists. Through his self-imposed exile from Franco's Spain he demonstrated the indissoluble link between artistic and political freedom. Aside from his activities as soloist, he was also a great chamber music player; and from time to time he filled the role of conductor, composer and teacher.

Pianist and harpsichordist, Wanda Landowska was one of the musicians primarily responsible for the resurgence of interest in early music, and particularly in the harpsichord and its repertoire. Although she toured widely, she was equally well known as a teacher, recording artist and scholar. Landowska remains the most influential woman instrumentalist of the century.

Vladimir Horowitz's phenomenal technique and questionable musicianship have made him the most controversial pianist of our time; and his personal eccentricities and extended periods of withdrawal from the concert platform seem only to have enhanced his audience appeal. In many ways, he is a throwback to a bygone age of sheer dazzling virtuosity.

Glenn Gould, who was born 150 years after Paganini, represents a completely opposing point of view on musical performance – one so drastic that it in fact considers the giving of concerts to be immoral. He has devoted most of his performing career exclusively to making records and has not given a public concert since 1964. His performances are a mixture of brilliant originality and seemingly gratuitous perversity. From the wandering virtuoso-as-audience-subduer of Paganini, we have reached the virtuoso-as-anchorite of Gould – the latest and most puzzling development in this history.

There is one clear and very important dividing point in the material, and it occurs between the third and fourth chapters – between Rubinstein and Paderewski. Paganini, Liszt and Rubinstein left no audible traces of their art as performers; but from Paderewski onwards, we have substantial documentation in the form of recordings. Obviously, the nature of a book changes when the author can contribute his own opinions. Nevertheless, as wide and as reliable a range of viewpoints as possible has been assembled for the purpose of examining the playing of both pre-recording-era and later performers. Most musicians will in any case agree that some mysterious process causes certain records to change – tempi, dynamics, everything – as they sit unplayed on the shelves, and that when one returns to them after having set them aside for a few years one discovers details great and small which could not possibly have sounded the same a few years earlier. I expect that if I re-read this book in ten years' time, I shall find many of my current opinions as incomprehensible as I now find some of those I held ten years ago.

H.S., Loro Ciuffenna, January 1982

Chapter One

Niccolò Paganini

❖❖❖❖❖❖❖❖❖❖❖❖❖❖❖❖❖❖❖❖❖❖❖❖❖❖❖❖❖❖❖❖❖❖❖❖

THE EXPRESSION *Paganini non si ripete* is a common one in Italy; it means that a Paganini comes but once and, by extension, that genius is inimitable. The adage is symptomatic of the career and legend of Niccolò Paganini. People in Italy and elsewhere who have even the slightest familiarity with European musical history have heard something of that legend, of Paganini's wild life as a lover and gambler, of the belief held by some nineteenth-century listeners and writers that there was something super-natural and literally diabolical in his playing. Stendhal, who heard Paganini in Milan before the violinist had played outside of Italy, reported to the French-speaking public in all seriousness that 'this ardent soul did not develop his sublime talent through eight years of patient conservatory study, but as a consequence of an error in love, which, it is said, caused him to be thrown into prison for many years. Alone and abandoned . . . nothing remained to him but his violin. He learned to translate his soul into sounds, and the long evenings of confinement gave him the time to perfect himself in that language.'[1] And the critic of the sober *Leipziger Musikalische Zeitung* stated in 1829, when Paganini was at last playing, and with the most extraordinary success, all over Europe: 'This man, with his long black hair and pale face, opens to us through sound a world that we may have experienced before, but only in dreams. There is something so demonic in his appearance that at one moment we seek the "hidden cloven hoof", at the next, the "wings of an angel".'[2]

What is most remarkable in all this is that Paganini himself encouraged the dissemination of these tales with the nonchalant adroitness of a masterly twentieth-century press agent – or at least that was true until he had become the most madly idolized instrumentalist in history. At that point, he tired of giving the devil more than his due and demanded to be recognized as an original and very diligent genius, rather than the tool of a super-natural force. But it was too late: he had become the victim of his own successful publicity; and no matter how many calmly explanatory letters he sent to musical journals, disclaiming the nonsense about him that abounded in the press, he remained for many a phenomenon that could not be described in material terms. As a result, the well-known violinist and pedagogue Carl Flesch was forced to write, a century later, that despite Paganini's 'thirty-odd years of concert giving, we chiefly have to rely on feuilletonistic gush from raving newspaper reporters or else on fantasies of undoubted literary value which, however, are beneath factual discussion. . . . Concerning his style, then, we are completely in the dark; each of us has a different picture of this mysterious figure, so that our contemporary violin quacks may with impunity permit themselves to use Paganini's name as a signboard for their dubious reforms.'[3]

The situation is not quite as desperate today as it was when Flesch wrote those words a generation-and-a-half ago: so very much was written about Paganini, especially during the last dozen years of his life, that some of it inevitably turned out to be worthwhile. During the past half-century scholars such as Arturo Codignola and G. I. C. de Courcy have been able to organize and publish a great deal of valuable information on Paganini. Others like Maria Tibaldi Chiesa and Michelangelo Abbado have analyzed the material and have made some worthwhile deductions about Paganini's way of playing the violin.

But one must forgive, at least in part, even the gush-producers, for it is clear that nothing even vaguely resembling the Paganini phenomenon had ever appeared before. The normally sensible Castil-Blaze, music critic of the *Journal des Débats*, summarized Paganini's first Paris concert in these words: 'It is the most astonishing, surprising, marvellous, miraculous, triumphant, dumbfounding, unheard-of, singular, extraordinary, incredible, unexpected thing.'[4] And the precise critic of London's *Athenaeum* admitted contritely that he had not believed all he had heard about Paganini before the violinist's arrival in Britain. 'Nay, last year we ventured to back de Beriot against him; we here retract. De Beriot is a sweet, chaste player – but Paganini is a solitary man in his art! There is a relation between a unit and a million – none between him and his fellow men.'[5] A great many observers were disorientated by Paganini: they had no vocabulary to describe what they saw and heard or their own reactions to it. Even Goethe was disconcerted: 'I lack a base for this column of sunbeams and clouds. I heard something simply meteoric and was unable to understand it.'[6]

16

Strictly speaking, it would be incorrect to assert that Paganini was a completely original figure who had no artistic forbears. It is well known that genius is in the first place an unusually great capacity for synthesizing the fruits of others' efforts. But in another sense he was indeed a self-engendered prototype. Others before him had discovered interesting effects on the violin, just as others before him had played the instrument with emotional intensity. No one, however, had explored and developed its technical capacities with anything approaching Paganini's maniacal thoroughness; and it appears that no one had played it with such a kaleidoscopic variety of expression. Corelli had been famous for his singing tone quality, Vivaldi for his technical brilliance (including placing his fingers 'but a hair's breadth from the bridge, so that there was barely room for the bow, doing this on all four strings with imitations at incredible speed'),[7] Geminiani for his double-stopping and shifting, Tartini for his elegant bowing, Viotti for his musical sensitivity; but Paganini accomplished all this and much, much more. His personality, too, was so strange and so strong that it added a powerful measure of non-musical fascination to his entire operation. For these reasons, the history of the modern virtuoso begins with Paganini. The Dionysian, audience-stupefying aspects of the careers of subsequent virtuosi were derived from the Paganini phenomenon; and even those artists in this book whose music-making seems to have little in common with Paganini's – Kreisler, Casals, Landowska, Gould – will be seen to owe him a great deal. While it is a straightforward enough task to appreciate and judge their work, according to one's tastes, on the basis of that work alone, it is not possible to gain a perspective on their various achievements without coming to an understanding of Paganini's.

Not until he was in his mid-forties, when his international career was beginning, did Paganini start to give somewhat detailed accounts of his childhood and studies. Needless to say, they are not entirely reliable. It was, in fact, in Vienna in 1828 that writers began to approach him for information; and de Courcy believes that some of his tales of paternal oppression and forced practice were influenced by stories he was told about his great idol,

Beethoven, who had died in that same city only a year earlier. Nevertheless, something substantial can be drawn from it all.

Paganini was born in Genoa on 27 October 1782. His father, Antonio, was a dock worker and shipping clerk who was able to support his family decently though certainly not in great comfort. Antonio Paganini was a fanatical amateur musician who played the mandolin and violin; his wife, Teresa Bocciardo, was also very fond of music. Niccolò* began to receive instruction on the mandolin at the age of five and on the violin two years later. He claimed later in life that his father went so far as to withhold food from him to make him practise more, and that his health suffered as a result. We know that he was a sickly child, and an even sicklier adult; but after only three years of violin studies with his father and local teachers, he was performing in public. When he was thirteen his father took him to Parma to study with the famous Alessandro Rolla, who, however, after hearing the boy once, told him that he had nothing to teach him and sent him to Ferdinando Paër and Paër's pupil Ghiretti for lessons in composition. Paganini spent most of 1796 and 1797 in Parma and even gave concerts there. During the last few years of the century he also met and heard two well-known violinists who visited Genoa: a Pole named Duranowski, from whom he learned many technical tricks, and the Frenchman Rodolphe Kreutzer, to whom Beethoven later dedicated his most famous sonata for violin and piano. But as was to be the case with Liszt at the piano and Casals at the cello, Paganini's violin-playing was obviously original nearly from the start. A glimpse of this can be caught from his statement to Schottky, his first biographer, concerning one of his early Genoese teachers, Giacomo Costa:

I recall with pleasure the good Costa's attentiveness which, however, did not give me particular satisfaction, in that his principles often seemed unnatural to me; and I did not condescend to adopt his method of drawing the bow. . . . I myself was enthusiastic about my instrument and studied incessantly to discover altogether new and unheard-of positions, the sound of which astounded people.[8]

Paganini began very early to conceive of the violin in an entirely different way than anyone before him had done; and nothing provides clearer evidence of this than his famous *Twenty-four Caprices* for violin solo, which he is believed to have

---

* This was the most common spelling of his name, although he himself occasionally spelled it Nicolò or even Nicola.

begun writing when he was still in his teens. These pieces are a whole school of violin-playing in themselves – and what violin-playing! They require a technical mastery that few have ever achieved. Today the *Caprices* are referred to with distaste by some musicians, and it is undeniable that they are hard to stomach when played unexceptionally. In Paganini's own hands they must have sounded extraordinary, not only because his technique was ironclad, but quite simply because he had the ability to make everything he played sound extraordinary. He had never intended the *Caprices* to be profound spiritual revelations; so it is all the more significant that Brahms, many years after Paganini's death, called them 'a great contribution to musical composition in general and to the violin in particular.'[9] Furthermore, it often happens that when a great performing musician throws all his energies into realizing a work whose spiritual value is small, the interpretation becomes a work of art in itself and elevates what it interprets. That is because the material challenges become in themselves spiritual problems. Certainly this was the case with Paganini's art. Ignaz Moscheles, one of the most highly-regarded pianists of his day and a disciple of Beethoven, heard Paganini in London in 1831 and remarked in his diary: 'Had that long-drawn, soul-searching tone lost for a single second its balance, it would have lapsed into a discordant cat's-mew; but it never did so. . . . His compositions were so ultra-original, so completely in harmony with the weird and strange figure of the man, that, if wanting in depth and earnestness, the deficiency never betrayed itself during the author's dazzling display of power.'[10]

Until the age of eighteen Paganini was kept quite firmly under his father's watchful eye; but in 1801 he left Genoa and went to Lucca, where his playing quickly attracted attention. The Abbé Jacobo Chelini reported disapprovingly on Paganini's début appearance, which took place during a solemn Pontifical mass in the Cathedral on 14 September. His account gives an interesting picture not only of the violinist's tricks at the beginning of his career, but also of the revolutionary and anti-clerical feelings which gripped much of Italy during the Napoleonic period:

. . . The Government wished this excellent violinist to exhibit his musical ability but since the Motet at the Epistle and another concerto at the Offertory gave him no opportunity to play during the celebration of the Mass, the Minister of the Interior . . . gave orders (contrary to all

19

regulations) that Paganini was to play a violin concerto at the conclusion of the Kyrie, and he was indiscreet enough to play one that took fully twenty-eight minutes. This professor certainly manifested an unusual and unprecedented ability and virtuosity. He imitated on his strings the songs of birds, the flute, trombone and horn, and though everyone admired his astounding bravura, when they heard such mimicry produced on a violin, it nevertheless aroused laughter even in church. . . . He was also able to play a whole concerto on one string. . . . He lacked judgment and self-criticism because to imitate on the violin the songs of birds and the tones of other instruments certainly shows a great ability but, being only mimicry, it is merely youthful caprice and should be performed at a concert in a theatre, but not in a sacred edifice. However, the concerto received great applause, like all the music, the Jacobins leading the ovation. They said that such music had never before been heard at a Santa Croce celebration, and if anyone had dared to criticize it, he ran the risk of being arrested. [11]

This and other successful appearances led to Paganini's appointment as leader of the Republic of Lucca's newly-founded national orchestra. In addition to teaching, playing and composing, his work there included conducting operas. He became deeply interested in the lyric repertoire (Cimarosa's *Il matrimonio segreto* was among the works he conducted); and the experience must have helped him to achieve the sustained, singing tone for which, among other things, he later became famous. Not long after Princess Elisa Baciocchi, Napoleon's sister, had become the ruler of Lucca and Piombino (1805), Paganini was made solo violinist to the court. It is generally held that he was also the Princess's lover for a time, although he had affairs with other women as well during his years in Lucca. One of them was his pupil Caterina Calcagno; another was Eleonora Quilici, in whose parents' home he had been a boarder. He maintained a lifelong affection for Eleonora, often giving financial help to her family, and even remembering her in his will. But he also contracted syphilis at an early age and was tormented intermittently by its debilitating effects for the rest of his life.

By the end of 1809 his responsibilities in Lucca had been reduced to such a point that he determined to leave altogether. For the next eighteen years he performed as a free artist throughout the Italian peninsula, astonishing audiences everywhere. Boucher de Perthes heard him at Livorno (Leghorn) in 1810 and wrote to his father:

I've told you of an Italian with whom I made music at Prince Baciocchi's. He's just been giving some concerts here, which have been a mad success. He's a Genoese by the name of Paganini, and is self-taught; therefore, he plays like nobody else. But he spoils his playing by buffooneries unworthy of the art and his fine talent. I've heard him add a cadenza to a concerto of Viotti's in which he imitates a donkey, a dog, a rooster, etc. Sometimes, at the beginning of a number, one of the strings breaks. You think he's going to stop but he goes right on playing on three strings. Then he plays variations on the G string. Where he excels is in his arpeggios, multiple stopping, and a pizzicato that he produces with the left hand. He then performs a mélange of all these things. It is enough to make you lose your mind! . . . When he leaves the theatre, three hundred people follow him to his hotel. He plays the guitar no less brilliantly than the violin and sings when he is among a few friends. But this isn't his strong point. He has a voice that would crack a pot.'

Paganini's Milan début at La Scala in the autumn of 1813 was an important moment in his career: it not only secured his fame and fortune in Italy, but also brought his name to the attention of musicians beyond the Alps. The Hungarian musician Peter Lichtenthal sent a report to Leipzig's *Allgemeine Musikalische Zeitung* that must have made German violinists either dismiss the story as a lie or wish to pawn their most precious possessions in order to travel to hear their Genoese colleague:

In a sense, he is without question the foremost and greatest violinist in the world. His playing is truly *inexplicable*. He performs certain passage work, leaps, and double stops that have never been heard before from *any* violinist, whoever he might be. He plays – with a special fingering of his own – the most difficult passages in two, three and four parts; imitates many wind instruments; plays the chromatic scale right close to the bridge in the highest positions and with a purity of intonation that is sheerly incredible. He performs the most difficult compositions on one string and in the most amazing manner while plucking a bass accompaniment on the others, probably as a prank. It is often difficult to believe that one is not hearing several instruments. . . . When it comes down to simple, deeply moving, beautiful playing, one can indeed find any number of violinists as good as he and now and then (and not infrequently at that) even some who certainly surpass him – Rolla for instance. . . . Musical connoisseurs are quite right in saying that he does not play the Kreutzer Concerto at all in the spirit of the composer, in fact, that he distorts much of it almost beyond recognition. On the other hand, his variations on the G string aroused universal admiration, for truly no one has ever heard anything to equal it. . . .[13]

21

As Paganini's fame increased, so did his troubles. His passion for gambling nearly ruined him; but after a particularly shattering experience in which he came close to losing his favourite violin, a Guarneri del Gesù, he was able to rid himself of the vice. One of his sexual liaisons brought disastrous consequences: the girl in question, Angelina Cavanna, was a minor, and her father brought two lawsuits against Paganini, both of which the violinist lost. His general state of health worsened, too. He was so gravely ill during 1822 and 1823 that he had to give up all concert activity. That activity was resumed in 1824, the same year in which he met a singer named Antonia Bianchi, who in 1825 bore him a son, Achille. (His relationship with Bianchi ended in 1828, and he thereafter assumed full responsibility for Achille.)

Finally, at the age of forty-five, Paganini made up his mind to give concerts outside of Italy. The results of this venture have no parallel in the history of music. More than a tour, it was a triumphal progress through Europe, a conquest not only of the mass public but also of serious musicians, who came away from his performances overwhelmed and confused.

His first stop was Vienna (spring and summer of 1828), where he had often been invited to appear. (One of his most fervent admirers in Austria was that well-known amateur violinist, Prince Metternich, who had first heard him in Rome some years earlier.) He was given honours, orders and titles by the Emperor, by other members of the aristocracy and by the city. Fellow musicians sought to visit him, to pay him homage, and noble families outdid each other to secure his presence at their soirées.

Paganini was delighted with his success and even astonished by its extent; but he never lost his shrewdness regarding audiences and finances. In a letter to a friend he reported: 'In order not to leave my money uninvested, I have delivered sixty thousand Austrian pounds to the Eskeles Bank. I have given my ninth concert at the Italian Opera House; and as soon as the announcement of it was posted all the boxes and single seats were sold. As a result I am forced to remain in Vienna all this month and the next, in order to give five or six more Academies. I have written two *Adagios* in double stops, which produce an effect.' And he adds with a touch of malicious humour: 'One made them cry, and the other, entitled "Religious", made the audience feel contrite.' Even his afternoon concerts in Vienna attracted too great a public to be accommodated, although the

Empress, various archdukes and archduchesses and other members of the court made sure to have places reserved for them. People generally took their seats fully two hours before the performances were to begin, in order to avoid any risk of losing places or of missing anything. One Viennese newspaper stated that Paganini's fame had reached such proportions that even the giraffe – a recently-arrived and newly-displayed gift from the Pasha of Egypt – had been consigned to second place in the minds of the citizenry.

From Vienna Paganini proceeded to Prague, where health problems again plagued him. An operation was performed on his jawbone and all his teeth were removed. By December he was able to resume his concert activities, and for the next two years he travelled through the various German states and Poland, creating everywhere an impression similar to the one he had achieved in Vienna. In Leipzig, the famed piano pedagogue Friedrich Wieck, father of Clara Schumann, noted in his diary (February 1829): 'Never have I heard a singer so moving as an Adagio played by Paganini. Never has an artist even been born who is as great and incomparable as he in so many genres.'[14] From Berlin a month later Mendelssohn wrote to his friend Moscheles: 'His never-erring execution is beyond conception. You ask too much if you expect me to give a description of his playing. It would take up the whole letter; for he is so original, so unique, that it would require an exhaustive analysis to convey an impression of his style.'[15] The young Chopin heard him in Warsaw in 1829 and was inspired to write a short piece, *Souvenir de Paganini*, in reminiscence of the event. Robert Schumann, then an unhappy nineteen-year-old law student at Heidelberg, journeyed to Frankfurt to hear Paganini the following spring and soon decided, partly as a result of the experience, to dedicate himself wholly to music. (He later transcribed for piano twelve of Paganini's *Caprices*, and named a section of *Carnaval* after the violinist.) The severe critic and theorist A. B. Marx commented that it was not so much Paganini's amazing technique as 'the inner poetry of his imagination'[16] that was so marvellous. 'Paganini is not himself,' said the poet and critic Ludwig Rellstab; 'he is rather joy, scorn, delirium and glowing pain . . . the sounds are only a means for him to express himself. . . .'[17]

Another musician, Carl Friedrich Zelter, Mendelssohn's teacher and Goethe's friend, wrote to the eighty-year-old poet (1829):

23

What the man achieves is extraordinary, and at the same time it must be noted that the effect of his playing is generally undesired and unachievable by other virtuosi on their instruments. His essence is thus more than music without being a higher music, and I daresay I would stand by this opinion if I heard him more often. I was in such a position that I could see all the movements of his hands and arms, since a rather small figure must in particular have suppleness, strength and elasticity. . . . [He is] like a clockwork with a soul. . . . He is in any case a perfect master of his instrument, at the height of his powers. . . .[18]

Paganini made a great impression on Heine, who heard him in Hamburg in 1830 and paid tribute to his evocative powers in *Florentine Nights*. It was also in Hamburg that an artist named Lyser made numerous drawings which are the best visual record extant of Paganini's playing. They show us, in addition, something of what Paganini's doctor and friend Francesco Bennati described in his *Notice physiologique*, written a year later. Bennati noted that Paganini was of average height and that 'his thinness and his lack of teeth, which gives him a sunken mouth and more prominent chin, make his physiognomy appear to be of a more advanced age. His large head, held up by a long, thin neck, appears at first glance to be rather strongly out of proportion to his delicate limbs.' This strange image was accentuated by his 'high, broad and square forehead, aquiline nose, ironic mouth . . . large and protuberant ears and black dishevelled hair, which contrasts with the pallor of his flesh. . . . The left shoulder is an inch higher than the right. . . .'[19] Bennati adds that although Paganini's hands were not larger than normal, they were exceptionally flexible.

Goethe read Bennati's findings in the *Revue de Paris* in 1831 and believed – as he wrote to Zelter – that they supported his theory that 'the organism produces and determines strange manifestations in living beings'.[20] While there is undoubtedly some truth in this theory, it is equally clear that the converse is also true – that is, that characteristics such as Paganini's high left shoulder and flexible hands were caused by his years of violin-playing. They are noticeable physical traits in many violinists.

Lyser's drawings also show us something of Paganini's characteristic stance, his weight thrown slightly more to his left foot than to his right, and his right elbow usually kept close to his body – a technique that is no longer used today.

It was during Paganini's travels in Germany that he met a

young woman named Helene von Dobeneck, daughter of a nobleman. She not only fell completely in love with Paganini: she was obsessed by him, and even converted to Catholicism in the hope of marrying him. He, however, does not appear to have been very interested in her. Eventually, her passion for him became a form of madness; and when he died she entered a convent, where she remained until her death at an advanced age. Paganini arrived in Paris in February 1831. In some respects, his début there on 9 March was the climax of his career. The audience included not only the cream of French aristocratic society, but also some of the most important figures in nineteenth-century culture. Among the violinists present were Pierre Baillot de Sales and Charles de Beriot; other musicians included Rossini, Donizetti, Liszt, Auber, Halévy and Maria Malibran; and Heine, de Musset, Théophile Gautier, Delacroix, George Sand, Jules Janin and Alphonse Kerr were also in the theatre. Their reactions were, by then, predictable. 'I never saw or heard anything to equal it in all my life', said Ludwig Boerne. 'The people have all gone crazy and will make everybody else crazy.'[21] Castil-Blaze, cited earlier, wrote: 'Sell all you possess, pawn everything, but go to hear him! Woe to those who let the opportunity go by! Let women bring their newborn babies so that sixty years hence they can boast of having heard him!'[22] Elsewhere he gave the opinion that it would be impossible for quite a while thereafter for any other violinist to establish any sort of reputation. 'There is no comparison possible between him and the others who have gone before him.'[23] For Delacroix, Paganini incarnated the ideal of artistic mastery: 'There was an inventor,' he mused in his Journal a quarter-century later; 'there was the right man for the right job. I was thinking of so many artists who are the opposite, in painting, in architecture, in everything.'[24]

Paganini does not seem to have been very interested in the intellectual and artistic life which Paris offered, although he clearly appreciated the tributes of its leading figures. He may have been a cunning man, but he was not a pretentious one: it was not in his nature to feign interest in people or subjects that meant nothing to him. The young Liszt plunged deeply into all that Paris had to offer; Paganini simply gave a dozen concerts there in two months and then moved on to the next town. His three great passions, at least at that time, were his art, women and the amassing of a secure fortune.

The last of these preoccupations caused him some serious

trouble during his stay in Paris. There as elsewhere, the price of a ticket to one of his concerts was exorbitant. While the public may not have been happy about that fact, no one was surprised by it, either. When, however, he refused an invitation to play for charity at a ball given by the National Guard, the press seized the occasion to demonstrate the idol's clay feet. Paganini was called an avaricious miser, and all sorts of defamatory stories about him began to circulate and to gain credence. The truth is that everywhere in his travels, Paganini had often given concerts for charity, and had intended to do so in Paris, too; but, quite understandably, he did not want to play at a policemen's ball. He defended himself by sending letters to the press, and he did eventually turn all the receipts of one of his performances over to various charitable institutions; but slander had already triumphed. For the rest of his days Paganini would hear himself labelled and libelled as a miser. Not only that: the French press also began to publish the old tales of Paganini's crimes, imprisonment and pacts with the devil – and this time the stories reached a mass public. With the help of F. J. Fétis, founder and publisher of the *Revue Musicale*, Paganini framed a reply that was duly published in that journal. In his letter Paganini said that there were 'several versions' of the story of his imprisonment:

It has been said, for instance, that having surprised my rival in my mistress's home, I bravely stabbed him in the back at the moment when he was unable to fight back. Others have insisted that my jealous fury was spent upon my mistress herself; but they do not agree as to the manner in which I brought her days to an end. Some say I used a dagger; others have it that I wanted to enjoy her sufferings by giving her poison. . . .

In this regard, here is what happened to me in Padua about fifteen years ago. I had given a concert there, and had been heard with some success. The next day, I was seated at the guest table among sixty others, and I had not been noticed as I entered the room. One of the diners expressed himself in flattering terms regarding the effect I had produced the previous evening. His neighbour joined his praises to the other's and added: 'There is nothing surprising in Paganini's skilfulness; he owes it to an eight-year stay in prison, where he had only his violin to lighten his captivity. He had been condemned to such a long detention for his cowardly murder of a friend of mine who was his rival.'

. . . I spoke up by addressing myself to the person who knew my story so well. I asked him to tell me when and where this adventure had taken place. . . . Imagine the astonishment when they recognized the leading actor in this tragic story! The narrator was much embarrassed. It was no longer his friend who had perished: he had heard it said – it had been stated – he had believed – but it was possible that he had been deceived. . . . People inclined to laziness do not wish to understand that one can study just as well in freedom and in one's own room as under lock and key.

Paganini goes on to describe an occurrence at the time of his Viennese successes:

One gentleman . . . stated that nothing in my playing astonished him, for while I was playing my variations he had clearly seen the devil next to me, guiding my arm and directing my bow. The resemblance between our features was sufficient evidence of my origin: he was dressed in red, had horns on his head and a tail between his legs. You will be able to understand, sir, that after such a detailed description there was not the least doubt as to the truth of the matter: therefore many people were convinced that they had come upon the secret of what are called my *tours de force*.

For a long time my peace of mind was disturbed by all these rumours that had been spread about me. I set about to demonstrate their absurdity . . . but something of it will always remain, and I was not surprised to find it here once again. . . . I see no other choice but to resign myself and to let this maliciousness go on at my expense. . . .[25]

The legend of Paganini's supernatural powers, the story created or at least encouraged by Paganini himself in earlier days, had grown beyond recognition and had generated similar tales, equally incredible. Denials and retractions were, as he had predicted, of no avail. Furthermore, when, after leaving France, he arrived in London for his first series of concerts in Britain, he found that *The Times* and other newspapers and journals had already been attacking him for his alleged greed. Nevertheless, his London début (3 June 1831) was a great event in the city's musical history. Moscheles, whose father-in-law had previously helped Paganini to obtain a very lucrative engagement in Germany, was visited several times by the violinist before that first concert. Paganini expressed what Moscheles considered to be exaggerated gratitude to the father-in-law and even 'took down from the mantlepiece a miniature portrait of his benefactor, covered it with kisses, and addressed it with the most high-flown epithets'. In his diary, Moscheles went on to describe those olive-tinted, sharply defined features, the glowing eyes, the scant but long black hair, and the thin, gaunt figure, upon which the clothes hung loosely, the deep sunken cheeks, and those long, bony fingers. . . . My assistance is of use to him here, and I am paid with quite as many honeyed epithets as my father-in-law received. . . . We receive him well, although I suspect he is rather too sweet to be genuine.

Of course Moscheles was present at the first concert:

The crowd in the opera house was wild with excitement. He had to play nearly everything twice over, and was not only greeted with vehement clapping of hands, but every lady leaned forward out of her box to wave her handkerchief at him; people in the pit stood up on the benches, shouting 'Hurrah! Bravo!' Neither Sontag nor Pasta [two great sopranos of the day] made such an impression here, much less any other artist. . . . Paganini's tone was always his own, and unique of its kind. The thin strings of his instrument, on which alone it was possible to conjure forth those myriads of notes and trills and cadenzas, would have been fatal in the hands of any other violin player, but with him they were indispensable adjuncts. . . .

After successive performances, Moscheles's opinion changed somewhat:

My mind is peculiarly vacillating about this artist. At first, nothing could exceed my surprise and admiration; his constant and venturesome flights, his newly discovered source of flageolet tones, his gift of fusing and beautifying subjects of the most heterogeneous kind; all these phases of genius so completely bewildered my musical perceptions, that for several days afterwards my head seemed on fire and my brain reeled. I never wearied of the intense expression, soft and melting like that of an Italian singer, which he could draw from his violin, and dazzled as I was, I could not quarrel with him for adopting the 'maniera del gatto' [cat's style], a term of opprobrium, showing how averse the Italians are to this style, which I dislike so intensely that I should only like to hear it once in every leap year. Suffice it to say, my admiration of this phenomenon, equally endowed by nature and art, was boundless. Now, however, after hearing him frequently, all this is changed; in every one of his compositions, I discover *the same* effects, which betrays a poverty of invention; I also find both his style and manner of playing mono-tonous. . . . I long for a little of Spohr's earnestness, Baillot's power, and even Mayseder's piquancy. . . . It may possibly be that the man, who grows more and more 'antipatico' to me every day, prejudices my judgment of the artist. He is so disgracefully mean. . . . Lablache offered

28

him £100 to play at his benefit, but Paganini refused, and the great singer had to allow him one-third of the receipts of his concert. When the Opera concerts . . . ceased to command full attention, he began a series in the London Tavern in the City. This was thought unworthy of a great artist; but it was all one to him, for he makes money there.[26]

What Moscheles fails to mention is that the famous basso Luigi Lablache was in no greater need of money than was Paganini; that the London Tavern was not simply a pub but a hall that seated eight hundred; that he did not accept any fee for two of his appearances – one for the benefit of orchestra musicians and their families, the other for London's orphans; and that he acceded to the request of some church musicians whose religious beliefs did not permit them to enter theatres, by arranging to play for them elsewhere. It is undeniable that Paganini was interested in money and demanded the highest fees that his public would pay; but as Moscheles and other detractors well knew, the same was true of the overwhelming majority of performing artists, great and small; and it is still true today.

Paganini himself seems to have been even more excited by the extent of his London success than he had been in Paris. He wrote to a friend:

If I wrote for a year [about the début concert] I would not manage to tell you the smallest part of it. The whole theatre, stalls, boxes and gallery, seemed a sea in a storm, as much for the noise of voices and hands as for the waving of handkerchiefs and the hats thrown in the air. They say things that I ought not to repeat: read them, if you can, and you will see. Everyone says unanimously that this sort of triumph is without precedent here; and it is all the more flattering to me in as much as it was necessary for me to destroy with the sound of my instrument the bad impression made on the public by the altered prices, which I had established for my concerts from the outset. I played, and all the mutterings were transformed into inexpressible praises. . . . The whole audience, as if by involuntary action, found itself standing on the benches and chairs in the stalls; above, in the boxes, you would have thought that they wanted to throw themselves down. . . . The enthusiasm was not contained within the walls of the Theatre: wherever I appear, on the streets or elsewhere, people stop, follow me, crowd around me. I shall repeat a phrase of the *Times*: 'You may not believe half of what I am telling you, and I am not telling you half of what there is to be told.' Now there are invitations here, invitations there, from the highest lords, and I don't know where to go first. . . .

By invitation of the King, I have played at Court, and I am awaiting a ring, since his jeweller came to measure my finger. . . .

A mass of portraits, done by various artists, has appeared in all the shops; each shows my features, more or less, but none has yet appeared among these prints that really resembles me. One also sees some funny caricatures; one shows me in the act of playing, in a strange position, while the music stand catches fire and burns; another in the act of embracing a beautiful lady – because of a rumour that had been spread according to which I had fallen in love with a very pretty English miss; a third in which I am playing the violin on one string, with a funny saying underneath; and another which portrays Lablache playing a bell, which he did in one of my concerts. I laugh myself to death and let them do as they please.

. . . The fifth concert was the most remunerative. An increasingly full house; hundreds of people were turned away and more than two hundred had to be satisfied with places among the orchestra players, whom I had put on stage in order to be able to sell tickets at a guinea each in the orchestra's usual position below. Never had such an attendance been seen in London. . . .[27]

Paganini played 112 concerts in the British Isles between the late spring of 1831 and the early spring of 1832, with the greatest success. One may legitimately question whether listeners in small English, Irish and Scottish towns at that time had any standards at all by which to judge even barely competent musicians, let alone Paganini; yet many people are sensitive to great intensity and to what is exceptional in other human beings. Artists who are willing to lay not just their reputations and self-esteem but also their souls on the line every evening at 8 pm are rare indeed, and professional musicians have no particular advantage over laymen in recognizing extraordinary spiritual wellsprings in their fellows. The critic of *The Observer* groped towards an understanding of the Paganini phenomenon when he described his first view of the violinist: 'Paganini was dressed in black, and wore the ribbon of an order. He played in the front of the stage, without any book, and when he accompanied the band, he did so wholly from memory. . . . His carriage may be called awkward, his bow and whole deportment ungainly, but there is a singularity in his manner which, though partaking of the grotesque, denotes a man of no ordinary stamp, and rivets the attention. . . .'[28] And Mary Shelley wrote to a friend that Paganini's playing 'threw me into hysterics. I delight in him more than I can express – his wild ethereal figure, rapt look – and the sounds he draws from his violin are all superhuman.'[29]

Then, suddenly, the decline began – the decline in Paganini's health, in his enthusiasm, in his playing and in his fortunes. He played in France and England in 1832, then for some reason gave no concerts at all for six months. When he did resume playing, his successes were far less stunning than in the past. In Paris in the autumn of 1833 he became seriously ill (pulmonary haemorrhage); however, in December he attended a performance of Berlioz's *Symphonie fantastique*. In his memoirs the composer wrote:

. . . a man waited for me alone in the hall, a man with long hair, a keen eye, a strange and ravaged face – a possessed genius, a colossus among giants, whom I had never seen, and the first glimpse of whom disturbed me deeply. He stopped me in the corridor in order to shake my hand, overwhelmed me with ardent praises which set fire to my heart and my head; it was Paganini!![30]

The violinist owned a Stradivari viola which he wanted to play in public, and he commissioned Berlioz to write a work for viola with orchestra. When he saw the newly-composed first movement, he was displeased. 'I am too long silent in it,' he said; 'I must play all the time.'[31] Berlioz went on, independently, to finish writing his great *Harold in Italy*; and when, five years later, Paganini heard the work played, he was greatly impressed by it. The next day Paganini's son brought Berlioz a letter from his father:

My dear friend
Beethoven is dead; only Berlioz could bring him back to life; and I, who have tasted your divine compositions, worthy of your genius, feel it my duty to beg you to accept, as a token of my homage, twenty thousand francs, which will be paid to you by my lord Baron de Rothschild after you have presented him with the enclosed [note]. Believe me always your affectionate friend
Nicolò Paganini.[32]

Surely there have been few such generous acts on the part of one musician towards another in the history of the art. With this money, Berlioz was able to pay his debts and to work at another of his masterpieces, *Romeo and Juliet*.

In 1834 Paganini played in Belgium, Holland, Britain and France, but again the results were not to be compared with those

31

of former years. He fell in love with the nineteen-year-old daughter of his English impresario. The girl, Charlotte Watson, appeared as vocal soloist in some of his concerts, and Paganini considered marrying her. But this intention, like so many similar ones over the years, came to nothing. He had recently purchased for himself a villa near Parma, and he now decided to bring his career to a close and to retire there. For a brief period he success- fully conducted the court orchestra of Marie Louise, Grand Duchess of Parma, sister of the Austrian Emperor and Napoleon's widow; but his plans for the ensemble were too ambitious to please many court councillors, and he resigned after only a few months. Late in 1836 and early in 1837 he gave a few violin concerts in the south of France, then returned to Paris where he had invested his money in a gambling establishment, the Casino Paganini. That venture failed the following year. Karl Halle, a young German pianist and conductor who was later, as Charles Hallé, to play an important role in England's musical life, saw Paganini during that unhappy period.

The striking, awe-inspiring, ghost-like figure of Paganini was to be seen nearly every afternoon in the music shop of Bernard Latte, Passage de l'Opéra, where he sat for an hour, enveloped in a long cloak, taking notice of nobody, and hardly ever raising his piercing black eyes. He was one of the sights of Paris, and I had often gone to stare at him with wonder until a friend introduced me to him, and he invited me to visit him, an invitation I accepted most eagerly. I went often, but it would be difficult to relate a single conversation we had together. He sat there, taciturn, rigid, hardly ever moving a muscle of his face, and I sat spellbound, a shudder running through me whenever his uncanny eyes fell upon me. . . . [33]

Paganini's health continued to decline, and he spent his last months in the south of France. His physical sufferings were great and he brooded over the many disillusionments which life had brought him. On 7 January 1840 he wrote to Berlioz: 'It is all over, now; envy can only be silent.'[34] On 27 May he died in Nice at the age of fifty-seven. To the end, he had refused the sacraments of the Church; and although his family and friends claimed that this was because he did not believe he was about to die, the archbishop was probably correct in judging that Paganini was in fact a non-believer. A long and macabre battle began over the question of whether or not he could be buried in sanctified ground, and for five years his lead coffin was kept in a basement.

In 1845 he was buried at his villa in Parma, and his remains now occupy a place of honour in Parma's main cemetery.

The mystery of Paganini's playing was of course no mystery at all, but rather an unprecedented ability to master every form of violin technique known up to his time, to perfect new techniques undreamt of by his predecessors or contemporaries and, above all, to play with irresistible beauty and expressiveness. Fétis, in his celebrated *Biographie universelle des musiciens*, described the Paganini operation as he had heard it at its peak:

The contrast of different sonorities, the varied ways of tuning the instrument, the frequent use of single and double harmonics, the effect of combining pizzicato with bowed notes, the different types of staccato, the use of double and even triple stops, a prodigious ease in performing wide intervals perfectly correctly, and finally, an unheard-of variety of bowing accentuations – these were the means which, combined, formed the physiognomy of Paganini's talent; and they were means which drew their value from . . . an exquisite nervous sensitivity and great musical feeling.[35]

His unusual techniques were many. He would often tune all four strings a semitone sharp in order to produce a more brilliant sound. In his pieces for one or two strings only he sometimes placed the G string in the A string's normal position; and he had a three-octave range on the G string – which means that he shifted all the way to the bridge, thanks to the abnormal flexibility of his fingers. Michelangelo Abbado points out that in Paganini's variations on *God Save the King* there are 'melodies and double-stops played with the bow while the left hand plucks the bass line; and, on the contrary, there are quick pizzicato notes and [pizzicato] trills on the E string, played by the left hand alone, while the bow accompanies by holding long notes on the open D or G string.'[36] Abbado adds that it is known that Paganini played his *Sonata à mouvement perpetuel* in Paris in 1832 at a tempo of ♩ = 184, or twelve notes per second!

As his career proceeded, Paganini gradually adopted thinner strings than normal in order to obtain purer harmonics. His hands were amazingly supple and, according to Fétis, he could touch the centre of his left palm with the tip of his thumb. His sound was extremely loud only for special effect. He appears to have been the first violinist to have made regular use of artificial harmonics; and he played them 'with marvellous facility in all positions'.[37] Guhr, one of Paganini's earliest and most intelligent followers, states that 'only in arpeggios, which he plays vigorously – using the lower part of the bow and playing close to the bridge – does he raise his elbow and forearm a little, moving them away from his body.' He generally played staccato with the lower part of the bow, 'holding it with the thumb and index finger only. Still more often, he lets us hear a surprising and absolutely unique type of staccato. He throws the bow at the string, makes it rebound and runs through the scale with incredible rapidity, so that the notes seem to roll off like so many pearls.'[38] His fingerings, too, were most unorthodox, and he even crossed one finger over another. Abbado says:

His own works demonstrate the definitive development he gave to violin technique, even influencing indirectly the techniques of other instruments. Even today these works constitute a touchstone for the most battle-hardened violinists. . . .[39]

It is not possible here to discuss Paganini's compositions – the concerti, caprices, chamber music (including works for guitar, another instrument which he played very well) and so on. Few of them are played today, probably because their technical difficulties are often much greater than their musical substance. And let us not suppose that Paganini would disagree with this estimate of his work: after all, he was one of the first to try to penetrate the language of Beethoven's late quartets and one of the first to recognize the genius of Berlioz. He knew perfectly well who he himself was and what his contribution was. His expansion of violin technique made it possible for composers more gifted than himself to require more of people who performed their works.

Dazzling technique, great intensity of expression and a desire to impress the public as it had never been impressed before – these were the essential characteristics of Paganini's career. They also mark the path through the rest of this book; for Paganini was an original figure who created new attitudes and new expectations. The development of and reaction against those attitudes and expectations continue to extend in a great many directions down to our own day.

Chapter Two

Franz Liszt

❖❖

PAGANINI'S Paris début on 9 March 1831 made an extraordinary impression on a great many people. But there was one young man in the audience that evening who was so overwhelmed, so shaken by the experience that it altered the course of his life.

At the age of nineteen, Franz Liszt was already widely admired as a pianist in Vienna, Paris, London and other European musical centres; yet the encounter with Paganini's art seems to have given him both an intimation of his own potential and the determination to realize it. He set himself the goal of doing for and with the piano what Paganini had done for and with the violin. Each day, he informed a friend, he practised 'four or five hours of exercises (thirds, sixths, octaves, tremolos, repeated notes, cadenzas, etc. etc.). Ah! provided I don't go mad you will find an artist in me . . . . "And I too am a painter," cried Michelangelo the first time he saw a masterpiece. . . . Though small and poor, your friend does not cease to repeat the great man's words ever since Paganini's last performance.'[1]

What emerged from this intense period of labour was a Liszt whose mastery of the keyboard was unparalleled in his day and remains – despite the lack of audible evidence – a paragon even in our own.

Like Paganini, his model, Liszt has become more than a legendary instrumentalist: he is a prototype, a stereotype, an apotheosis of the pianist as virtuoso. His impact was so great that it is common even today to accept his supremacy on faith. 'A mere pianist he is not,'[2] said Mendelssohn. Moscheles, his senior colleague, wrote of Liszt when the latter was only sixteen that his playing 'surpasses in power and mastery of difficulties everything I have ever heard.'[3] Schumann claimed that he had 'never found any artist, except Paganini, to possess in so high a degree as Liszt this power of subjugating, elevating, leading the public.'[4] 'Such marvels of executive skill and power I could never have imagined,'[5] said Hallé. And Anton Rubinstein declared: 'I and my like are but ordinary soldiers beside that Field-Marshal,

Franz Liszt.'⁶ What is particularly interesting about these and similar comments is that they were made by important musicians of widely varying outlook, many of whom were wholly or partly opposed to Liszt's intentions and aesthetic point of view.

Liszt and the piano came of age at the same time. Although invented early in the eighteenth century and subsequently endowed with an imposing repertoire by composers like Carl Philipp Emanuel Bach, Haydn and Mozart, the instrument began to assume many of its present characteristics only in the first quarter of the nineteenth century. The use of metal in the frame increased; and Erard in Paris developed the double escapement, which allowed a key to be restruck without having first returned all the way to its rest-position. These and other changes were contemporary with Beethoven's transfiguration of European music. Pianists, like brass and woodwind players, were suddenly being called upon to execute passages which pushed their instruments' capabilities to the limit. At the same time the advances of the Industrial Revolution were making mechanical improvements possible, and these in turn facilitated certain aspects of execution. When Liszt was born (on 22 October 1811), the last great phase in the piano's development was already underway; by the time he was fifteen, the changes mentioned above had been achieved; and by mid-century, the piano was essentially the instrument we know today.

The village of Raiding, Hungary, was Liszt's birthplace. He was the son of a steward on the estates of Prince Eszterházy – scion of the same family which had employed Haydn for so many years. Adam Liszt provided his son with his earliest piano instruction; and by the age of nine the boy had so impressed some local barons who had attended his first public perform-ances that they undertook to support his studies for six years. He went to Vienna where, in addition to meeting Beethoven and Schubert, he studied composition with Salieri and piano with Beethoven's pupil, the famous pedagogue Carl Czerny. Czerny wrote in his memoirs:

I had never had so enthusiastic, brilliant and industrious a pupil. . . . It seemed necessary above all to use the first months to regulate and strengthen his mechanical dexterity in such a way that he could not possibly slide into any bad habits in later years. Within a short time he played the scales in all keys with a masterful fluency made possible

36

by a natural digital equipment especially well-suited for piano-playing. . . . Through intensive study of Clementi's sonatas . . . I instilled in him for the first time a firm feeling for rhythm and taught him beautiful touch and tone, correct fingering, and proper musical phrasing. . . . A few months later we took up the works of Hummel, Ries, Moscheles, and then Beethoven and Sebastian Bach. . . . Since I made him learn each piece very rapidly, he finally became such an expert sight-reader that he was capable of *publicly* sight-reading even compositions of considerable difficulty and so perfectly as though he had been studying them for a long time. Likewise I endeavoured to equip him with skill in improvising by frequently giving him themes to improvise on. . . . After only one year I could let him perform publicly, and he aroused a degree of enthusiasm in Vienna that few artists have equalled. . . .[7]

Czerny resented what he considered to be Liszt's premature departure from Vienna and from his own positive influence. Nevertheless, the boy's ambitious father took him to Paris, in order to have him study at the famous Conservatoire; there, however, the director, Cherubini, refused him admission on the grounds that he was a foreigner. But it hardly mattered: he had become a polished pianist by the age of twelve, and he was able to continue his composition studies privately. Paris remained his base for several years, although he toured England and Switzerland as well as France throughout the 1820s.

He was already a well-established figure in Parisian musical life when, in 1831, the Paganini phenomenon spurred him to more strenuous keyboard activity – challenged him, in a sense, to seek and follow the route of his destiny. The next few years were difficult and confusing for him, and for a time he became deeply interested in Saint-Simonism. During the same period, he and the Countess Marie d'Agoult met and fell in love; and in 1835 she abandoned her husband and child and ran off to Switzerland with Liszt. Three children were born of their relationship; the second, Cosima, married Liszt's gifted disciple, the pianist and conductor Hans von Bülow, and later left von Bülow to live with and eventually to marry Richard Wagner, her father's contemporary, whose career was also closely tied in with Liszt's.

Liszt's elopement with the Countess was an attempt to withdraw from the complicated, sophisticated Parisian life to which they both were accustomed. It was also a Romantic

37

protest, a challenge to conventional morality. Liszt moreover stood in awe of the Countess's superior general knowledge and broad culture, and he wished to improve himself under her tutelage and with her encouragement. In addition to offering the consolations of love, their secluded life together was to have embodied a whole gamut of ideals – some of them quite nebulous and no doubt understood diversely by each of the two parties. For a time, love held the whole parcel together; but since all of Liszt's efforts from childhood onwards had been geared towards conquering precisely the sort of society which the couple had left behind in fleeing Paris, it was inevitable that he, at least, should be drawn back to public life. The Countess was a gifted writer who later achieved a certain success as a novelist under the pseudonym of Daniel Stern. Her accounts, both fictionalized and in her journals, of her affair with Liszt expose what she considered to be weaknesses in his character; and a good deal of what she says seems unopposable. But Liszt, as we shall see, was unarguably a very great performer; and the desire, the need to demonstrate one's achievements before an audience is an important factor in most performers' personalities. Liszt did not merely want to *become* a better and more refined person: he also wanted to *show* how much better and more refined he had become. One may not like that aspect of the man; but it is a very strange tool for historians today to use for flaying him. Would anyone be writing about him a century after his death had that part of his make-up not been so strong?

As his affair with the Countess was coming to an end, his reputation as a pianist was reaching its apogee. For it was in 1839 that he returned to Paris to meet, with overwhelming success, the challenge offered by another extraordinary virtuoso, Sigismund Thalberg, to his keyboard supremacy. During the following eight years, Liszt's reputation as the greatest of all piano virtuosi was cemented. He proceeded from triumph to triumph throughout Europe, exciting the hysterical admiration of the mass public and a strange sort of wonderment mixed with contempt in many musicians and critics. The Viennese critic Eduard Hanslick attended Liszt's performances in the Austrian capital in 1846; many years later he described a typical Liszt recital of that period. Liszt, he said, generally dispensed with the traditional concert format, which included a mixture of solo pieces, orchestrally-accompanied numbers and music played or sung by secondary performers. Instead, he gave a solo recital, in the modern sense of the word; and in addition, while he rested between one work and the next, he would chat charmingly with the distinguished ladies who had bought places on the stage near the piano. His playing, said Hanslick,

was sometimes uneven, alternately good and bad; but it was always Liszt, and that was sufficient. The fact that it was influenced by the mood of the moment raised it only the higher in the esteem of the public, which was tired of the correct and dependable playing of the virtuoso who had gone before. . . .

In Liszt's apartment in the hotel 'Zur Stadt London' the younger musical generation of Vienna was in more or less continuous convention. He himself sat talking and smoking at the piano in a black velvet blouse, correcting proof sheets, or writing down some composition or other, the manuscript paper on his knee. . . . Ferdinand Hiller [German composer, pianist and conductor], in his interesting book on Mendelssohn, tells how the composer met him one day and cried: 'I have just seen a miracle! I was with Liszt at Erard's and showed him the manuscript of my concerto. He played it at sight – it is hardly legible – and with the utmost perfection. It simply can't be played any better than he played it. It was miraculous!' To which Hiller added the perceptive observation that Liszt commonly played any given piece best at the first reading; it was only then that it sufficiently occupied him. At a second playing he had to elaborate in order to make it interesting. . . .[8]

But what musicians thought of Liszt the pianist is so closely tied in with what they thought of the other aspects of his extraordinary life and career that one must try to look at the rest before examining his impact as a virtuoso.

When he was not busy touring, Liszt lived in Paris and at a very fast pace. His love affairs were so scandalous that they enhanced still further his reputation as an impetuous romantic virtuoso. Among his mistresses was Marie Duplessis, who had served as the model for *La Dame aux camélias* – written by one of her earlier lovers, Alexandre Dumas *fils* – and therefore, indirectly, also as the model for Violetta Valéry in Verdi's *La traviata*. Another was Lola Montez who, as mistress to the King of Bavaria, dipped into that kingdom's treasury just as expertly as Wagner was to do when a new king came under his influence a generation later.

Liszt also had an affair with Marie Pleyel, wife of the well-known piano manufacturer; and this created a rift between Liszt and Chopin. Once, while Chopin was away, Liszt used his friend's apartment as a place for meeting Madame Pleyel; and Chopin, who was a friend of her husband, was angered at having been drawn into the complicated situation. (Chopin once wrote that he would have liked to have stolen from Liszt 'the way to play my own Studies';[9] but he seems in general to have been repelled by Liszt's personality and to have intensely disliked his compositions.)

Liszt's literary friends and acquaintances included Balzac, Sue, Heine, Gautier, George Sand and Lamartine. He was very fond of Lamartine's poetry, and for a time also of Lamartine's niece, the Countess Valentine Cessiat, to whom he proposed in 1845. She rejected him.

By the time he reached his mid-thirties Liszt had amassed a considerable fortune and was able to contemplate giving up the hectic life of a wandering virtuoso and full-time public idol. Weariness was not, however, the only factor, or even the most important one, in his decision. First, there was the Princess Carolyne von Sayn-Wittgenstein. This Polish-born writer, religious mystic and *grande dame* abandoned her husband, a Russian prince, and his estate with its 30,000 serfs to live with Liszt and to try, like the Countess d'Agoult before her, to exert upon him what she considered to be a positive influence. In 1848 they settled in Weimar, that amazing little German duchy whose name had been made known around the world through Goethe's dominating presence during the first three decades of the century. Liszt had been an important figure in Weimar's musical life since 1842, playing and conducting concerts. (By all accounts, his exceptional musicianship and communicative abilities made him a formidable conductor.) But it was not until 1848 that he agreed to accept the position of conductor of Weimar's Court Opera. This was the second important reason for his rejection of the life of the travelling 'commercial virtuoso'. (After 1847 he never played the piano for remuneration.) It was his intention to support the finest talent of his day and to resurrect important works of the past which had fallen into oblivion. Thus operas such as Wagner's *Lohengrin*, Schumann's *Genoveva* and Schubert's forgotten *Alfonso und Estrella* received their first performances under Liszt's direction; two other operas by Wagner (*The Flying Dutchman* and *Tannhäuser*) and Berlioz's *Benvenuto Cellini* were given important early revivals; and many other works, great and small, were also produced.

1. Niccolò Paganini (1782–1840) as sketched by Sir Edward Landseer,
RA, after one of the violinist's London appearances, *c.* 1831. Note his
gaunt, dishevelled appearance, asymmetrical stance and low right
elbow – all of which correspond to contemporary reports.

2. (*Left*) Ingres's portrait of Paganini, 1819. His appearance is self-possessed and certainly not diabolical. There is a mysterious detail, however: although all four of the violin's strings are properly strung, a broken fifth string is hanging from the scroll. 3, 4, 5. (*Above, left*) Paganini caricatured in a lithograph, after the bronze statuette by Jean-Pierre Danton in the Musée Carnavalet, Paris. (*Right*) An engraving by R. Lane depicting the violinist's London début. (*Bottom*) The cover of a piece of popular music entitled 'Paganini's Dream', showing the violinist at a witches' sabbath.

6, 7. By the time Franz Liszt (1811–86) was thirteen years old – as shown in the portrait (*above*) – he had already played successfully in Vienna, Paris and London. He was embarking upon a career that was to establish a standard for pianists of several generations. (*Opposite*) Liszt's country-man Miklós Barabás depicted the pianist at the age of thirty-six and at the height of his fame. But it was in the same year that he determined to give up his life as a wandering virtuoso in order to settle in Weimar with his latest lover, Princess Carolyne von Sayn-Wittgenstein, and to devote himself to composing and to championing other composers' music.

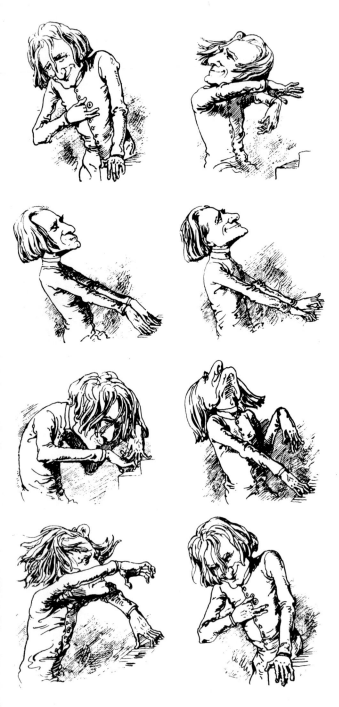

8. Franz Liszt, Sun-King of the piano, caught in several attitudes during the concert. Drawings by Jankó, from *Borsszem Jankó*, 6 April 1873.

Liszt appears in his cassock. Haughty smile. Hurricane of applause.

First chords. Turns around to force the audience to pay attention.

Closes his eyes and appears to be playing only for himself.

Pianissimo. St Francis of Assisi converses with the birds. His face is radiant.

Hamlet's self-questioning. Faust's torment. The keys exhale sighs.

Reminiscences: Chopin, George Sand, beautiful youth, fragrances, moon-beams, love.

Dante: the Inferno; the damned and the piano tremble. Feverish agitation. The hurricane breaks down the gates of Hell. – Boom!

He has only played for us – while trifling with us. Applause, shouts and hurrahs!

9. In the spring of 1886 Liszt visited London for the first time in forty-five years. His music was performed and he was even prevailed upon to play the piano at private gatherings. Sir Leslie Ward ('Spy') caricatured him – flowing white hair, warts and all – in a lithograph in *Vanity Fair*. Liszt died that summer, a few months before his seventy-fifth birthday.

10, 11. Anton Rubinstein (1829–1894) was the most celebrated pianist of the nineteenth century, Liszt excepted. An intelligent musician and a dedicated artist, he was responsible for three developments of lasting importance: he founded the St Petersburg Conservatory, thus preparing the way for the flowering of Russian musical life; he was one of the first major European musicians to undertake a lengthy American tour; and he gave throughout Europe a series of 'historical recitals' which covered three centuries of keyboard repertoire and which changed many pianists' thinking about the function of the recital itself. (*Left*) Rubinstein at the keyboard *c.* 1880. (*Below*) Rubinstein at Steinway Hall, New York, in 1872, with, among others, Theodore Thomas (*upper left*), Carlotta Patti (*second from left*) and Henri Wieniawski (*third from right*). (Caricature by Joseph Keppler)

Weimar moreover provided Liszt with an environment in which he was able to devote a great deal of time to composition. Twelve of his symphonic poems (a form which he invented), his *Faust* and *Dante* symphonies, his first piano concerto, a great number of original pieces for piano solo, songs, choral works and piano transcriptions of works by other composers date from the Weimar years.

It is legitimate to speculate on other motives behind Liszt's abandonment of the recital stage. By removing himself from the field of combat on which he had made his reputation, he was in effect stating that he stood apart from his colleagues – above and beyond them, above and beyond common criticism and, in short, in a class by himself. Still, his personal and professional generosity have been so widely attested that they more than outweigh his ego – which in any case was not so much king-sized as god-like, self-possessed and generally uninvidious.

From his sumptuous residence in Weimar's Altenburg palace, Liszt reigned with all the majesty of a prince of the blood. George Eliot and her companion George Henry Lewes visited him there in 1854; and in her letters and journal, the great novelist, who was also a great music lover, left interesting descriptions of both Liszt and the Princess.

(10 August, Journal) The appearance of the Princess rather startled me at first. I had expected to see a tall, distinguished woman, if not a beautiful one. But she is short and unbecomingly endowed with embonpoint; at the first glance the face is not pleasing, and the profile especially is harsh and barbarian, but the dark, bright hair and eyes give the idea of vivacity and strength. Her teeth, unhappily, are blackish too. She was tastefully dressed in a morning robe. . . . My great delight was to watch Liszt and observe the sweetness of his expression. Genius, benevolence and tenderness beam from his whole countenance, and his manners are in perfect harmony with it. . . . [Of a private Liszt performance at home:] I sat near him so that I could see both his hands and face. For the first time in my life I beheld real inspiration – for the first time I heard the true tones of the piano. He played one of his own compositions – one of a series of religious *fantaisies*. There was nothing strange or excessive about his manner. His manipulation of the instrument was quiet and easy, and his face was simply grand – the lips compressed and the head thrown a little backward. When the music expressed quiet rapture or devotion a sweet smile flitted over his features; when it was triumphant the nostrils dilated. There was nothing petty or egoistic to mar the picture. . . .

(16 August, letter to Charles Bray) . . . [Liszt] is a Grand Seigneur in this place, whereas Hofrath or Court Councillor is seldom anything more, as an Englishman would say, than a poor author. Liszt is extremely kind to us. . . . Liszt is the first really inspired man I ever saw. His face might serve as a model for a St. John in its sweetness when he is in repose but seated at the piano he is as grand as one of Michael Angelo's prophets.

(10 September, letter to Bessie Rayner Parkes) He has that 'laideur divinisée' by the soul that gleams through it, which is my favourite kind of physique. . . . (NB: George Eliot was herself 'divinely ugly'.)

(Autumn, Journal) About the middle of September the theatre opened, and we went to hear [Verdi's] 'Ernani'. Liszt looked splendid as he conducted the opera. The grand outline of his face and floating hair were seen to advantage as they were thrown into dark relief by the stage lamps. . . .[10]

Unfortunately, the enthusiasm of Weimar's court and public for Liszt's efforts on behalf of what he and Wagner called 'Music of the Future' began to wane after a few years, and Liszt, disillusioned, left Weimar in 1859. He felt that although there had been some individually successful productions, his attempts, viewed as a whole, had been a failure. Today it is clear that while the 'Weimar Project' may have been a short-term failure, its long-term influence – through the music of Wagner, Berlioz, Liszt himself and others – was enormous.

With the end of the Weimar sojourn came the end of the Princess Carolyne episode. She had been unsuccessful, a few years earlier, in her attempts to obtain a divorce from her husband; and her relationship with Liszt had subsequently cooled. He moved to the Villa d'Este near Rome, devoted himself to composition and religious meditation and, at the age of fifty-four, took minor orders in the Catholic Church.

Gregorovius saw him in Rome. 'He was getting out of a hackney carriage, his black silk cassock fluttering ironically behind him. Mephistopheles disguised as an Abbé. Such is the end of Lovelace.'[11] Gregorovius erred: the cassock did not put an end to Lovelace's activities. It was, in fact, during Liszt's Roman period that the maddest of his lovers, Olga Janina, came upon the scene. The fact that one of her pet leopards had killed the director of the Kiev Conservatory or that she had horse-whipped and abandoned her husband the day after their marriage did not seem to faze the Abbé. He was upset, however, when she aimed a loaded revolver at him during a particularly dramatic encounter in their unusual romance; but he managed to calm her, and was probably relieved when she disappeared from his life.

During the 1870s and 80s he returned to Weimar each year, giving what would today be called master classes in piano repertoire. Similar classes had been held during Liszt's permanent residence in Weimar; and among the more successful of the students who worked with him at one time or another were von Bülow, Karl Tausig, Felix Weingartner, Alexander Siloti, Moriz Rosenthal, Emil Sauer, William Mason, Karl Klindworth, Arthur Friedheim, Eugen d'Albert and Moritz Moszkowski. Having become a national hero in his native Hungary, he began to spend annual periods in Budapest. In 1875 he was elected president of the new Hungarian National Music Academy.

Occasionally, he gave benefit performances for various causes. Hanslick attended one in Vienna in 1874 and reported:

His playing was free, poetic, replete with imaginative shadings, and, at the same time, characterized by noble, artistic repose. And his technique, his virtuosity? I hesitate to speak of it. It suffices to observe that he has not lost it but has rather added to it in clarity and moderation. What a remarkable man! After a life incomparably rich and active, full of excitement, passion, and pleasure, he returns at the age of sixty-two and plays the most difficult music with the ease and strength and freshness of youth. Not only does one listen with breathless attention to his playing; one also observes its reflection in the fine lines of his face. His head, thrown back, still suggests something of Jupiter. Sometimes the eyes flash beneath prominent brows; sometimes the characteristically upturned corners of the mouth are raised even higher in a gentle smile. Head, eyes, and sometimes even a helping hand, maintain constant communication with the orchestra and audience. Sometimes he plays from notes, at other times from memory, putting on and taking off his spectacles accordingly. Sometimes his head is bent forward attentively, sometimes thrown back boldly. . . . For the Liszt of today it was a great accomplishment; and yet he went about it as if it were nothing, and he himself still the Liszt of 1840. A darling of the gods, indeed![12]

In 1886, the year of his seventy-fifth birthday, he was present at special performances of his works in England and France, despite his declining health; and that summer, he attended performances of *Parsifal* and *Tristan* at the Bayreuth Festival – then under the artistic directorship of his daughter, Cosima Wagner. It was at Bayreuth that he died on 31 July 1886.

It is not within the scope of this book to discuss Liszt's compositions. He was an extremely prolific composer, and a few of his works have enjoyed periods of popularity. After some rather lean decades, there now seems to be new interest in a greater number of his works than had ever before received serious attention. What is important here, however, is to bear in mind that Liszt associated himself most decidedly with the musical avant-garde of his day, and that that fact coloured, to some extent, the comments made about him and even about his playing by some of his contemporaries who sided with or against him.

Like Paganini, Liszt the virtuoso was an extraordinarily complicated individual. Today it is very difficult to separate the legend and lore of his pianism from its reality; in fact, since no recordings of his playing exist, the reality ceased to exist with Liszt's death.

The more amusing aspect of the legend is adequately represented by the following well-known description by Henry Reeves, an Englishman, of a Liszt concert in Paris in 1835:

Liszt had already played a great fantasia of his own, and Beethoven's twenty-seventh Sonata [Op. 90]. After this latter piece he gasped with emotion as I took his hand and thanked him for the divine energy he had shed forth. . . . [Liszt then played some of Mendelssohn's *Songs without Words*.] We had already passed that delicious chime of the Song written in a Gondola, and the gay tendrils of sound in another lighter piece. . . . As the closing strains began I saw Liszt's countenance assume that agony of expression, mingled with radiant smiles of joy, which I never saw in any other human face except in the paintings of Our Saviour by some of the early masters; his hands rushed over the keys, the floor on which I sat shook like a wire, and the whole audience was wrapped in sound, when the hand and frame of the artist gave way. He fainted in the arms of the friend who was turning over the pages for him, and we bore him out in a strong fit of hysterics. The effect of this scene was really dreadful. The whole room sat breathless with fear, till Hiller came forward and announced that Liszt was already restored to consciousness and was comparatively well again. As I handed Madame de Circourt to her carriage we both trembled like poplar leaves, and I tremble scarcely less as I write this. [13]

How much of this episode was real and how much of it invented by Mr Reeves is open to question; nevertheless, audiences of the

1830s and 40s expected emotional high jinks at Liszt's performances and, clearly, were satisfied.

On the other hand, the most respected musicians of the day took Liszt – or at least his playing – completely seriously; and there is no end to the testimony. Mendelssohn, for example, whose aesthetic principles were far more conservative than Liszt's, wrote to Moscheles from Leipzig in 1840:

Liszt has been here for the last six days. . . . His playing, which is quite masterly, and his subtle musical feeling, that finds its way to the very tips of his fingers, truly delighted me. His rapidity and suppleness, above all, his playing at sight, his memory, and his thorough musical insight, are qualities quite unique in their way, and that I have never seen surpassed. With all that, you find in him, when once you have penetrated beneath the surface of modern French polish, a good fellow and a true artist, whom you can't help liking even if you disagree with him. . . .[14]

Mendelssohn goes on to question Liszt's talents as a composer, then compares his playing to Thalberg's:

. . . Thalberg would meet with more success in many places – England, for instance. He, in his way, is just perfect; he plays the pieces he has mastered, and there he stops: whereas Liszt's whole performance is as unpremeditated, as wild and impetuous, as you would expect of a genius; but then I miss those genuinely original ideas which I naturally expect from a genius. . . .[15]

Moscheles himself, whose musical ideals were much closer to Mendelssohn's than to Liszt's, noted in his diary (London, 1841):

When [Liszt] came forward to play in Hummel's Septet, one was prepared to be staggered, but only heard the well-known piece which he plays with the most perfect execution, storming occasionally like a Titan, but still, in the main, free from extravagance; for the distinguishing mark of Liszt's mind and genius is that he knows perfectly the locality, the audience, and the style of music he brings before that audience, and uses his powers, which are equal to everything, merely as a means of eliciting the most varied kinds of effects.[16]

But in 1849 Moscheles wrote:

The tossing about of his hands, which he seems to think a mark of inspiration, I still regard as an eccentricity, although it is no doubt remarkable that he accomplishes the most perilous leaps with scarcely a single mishap.[17]

Friedrich Wieck heard Liszt in Vienna in 1838 and wrote in his diary:

He can be compared with no other pianist – he stands alone. He excites terror and astonishment and is a most lovable artist. His appearance at the piano is indescribable – he is original – he sinks into the piano. . . . His passion knows no bounds; not infrequently does he violate feelings of beauty by tearing the melody to pieces, by using the pedal too much, thereby making his compositions even more incomprehensible to the layman, if not to the connoisseur. His spirit is great; one can say of him, 'His art is his life'.[18]

And a few days later:

Weber's Conzertstück played by Liszt (at the beginning he broke three of the Conrad Graf's brass strings). Who can describe it? These missing bass-notes didn't embarrass him at all – he must be accustomed to it. What emotion to hear his playing and to be close to him. . . .

If he knew how to curb his strength and his fire – who could play after him? Thalberg has also written thus. And where are there pianos which can give back even half of what he is capable of and demands? . . .

Everything brilliant – the applause tremendous – the artist un-pompous and lovable – all new, unheard of – Liszt alone.[19]

Wieck's daughter Clara, later wife of Robert Schumann and herself one of the most esteemed pianists of the nineteenth century, wrote to her future husband at the time of Liszt's appearances in Vienna in 1840:

In his last concert but one, Liszt – with one chord – broke three hammers . . . and four strings as well. . . . Next to Liszt all virtuosi seem very small to me, even Thalberg. And myself – I can't even see myself anymore.[20]

Schumann himself heard Liszt in Leipzig during the same period and wrote to Clara:

He is really too extraordinary. His playing of the *Novelletten*, parts of the *Fantasie*, and the Sonata [all by Schumann], moved me strangely. Although his reading differed in many places from my own, it was always inspired, and he does not, I imagine, display such tenderness, such boldness, every day. . . .[21]

. . . Liszt seems to me more powerful every day. He played at R. Härtel's [music publisher] again early this morning – in a way that made us all tremble and rejoice – Chopin Etudes, a piece from Rossini's Soirées [musicales] and more besides.[22]

In his own publication, the *Neue Zeitschrift für Musik*, Schumann wrote of being 'overwhelmed by the flood of tones and feelings', and of the 'variety of wildness, tenderness, boldness, and airy grace. . . . He must be heard – and also seen; for if Liszt played behind the scenes, a great deal of the poetry of his playing would be lost. . . .'[23] Schumann did not like Liszt's transcription of the Scherzo and Finale from Beethoven's 'Pastoral' Symphony. But after a Dresden concert at which Liszt played works by three composers then resident in the town – Mendelssohn, Schumann and Hiller – Schumann commented:

Liszt played these pieces almost at sight; no one will be very well able to imitate him in this. He displayed his virtuosity in its fullest force, however, in the closing piece, the 'Hexameron', a cyclus of variations by Thalberg, Herz, Pixis and Liszt himself. Everybody wondered where he found the strength to repeat half of the 'Hexameron' and then his own galop. . . .[24]

Some years later Liszt appeared at the Schumann home in Dresden, playing to the hilt the role of the Great Man – at least according to Clara. He said that he found Schumann's Piano Quintet '*zu Leipzigerisch*'. Liszt detested Leipzig's famous Conservatory and the so-called 'academic' composers associated with it; and 'too Leipzig-like' in Liszt's jargon always meant 'unimaginative'. Then, according to Clara's diary, 'he played so shamefully badly that I was quite ashamed to have had to remain and not to have been able to leave the room. . . .'[25] Liszt visited the Schumanns again in 1851 and Clara wrote: 'He played as always with truly demonic bravura, he controls the piano truly like the devil (I cannot express it any other way . . .), but oh! his compositions – the stuff is really too awful!'[26]

Sir Charles Hallé first heard Liszt in the mid-1830s and later wrote of the experience in his memoirs:

I heard Liszt for the first time at one of his concerts, and went home with a feeling of thorough dejection. . . . He was a giant. . . . Chopin carried you with him into a dreamland, in which you would have liked to dwell forever; Liszt was all sunshine and splendour, subjugating his hearers with a power that none could withstand. For him there were no difficulties of execution, the most incredible seeming child's play under his fingers. One of the transcendent merits of his playing was the crystal-like clearness which never failed for a moment even in the most complicated and, to anybody else, impossible passages. . . . The power he drew from his instrument was such as I have never heard since, but never harsh, never suggesting 'thumping'. . . . If, before his marvellous execution, I had only to bow in admiration, there were some peculiarities of style, or rather of musicianship, which could not be approved. I was very young and most impressionable, but still his tacking on the finale of the C-sharp minor sonata (Beethoven's) to the variations of the one in A-flat, Opus 26, gave me a shock, in spite of the perfection with which both movements were played. Another example: he was fond at that time of playing in public his arrangement of the 'scherzo', 'The Storm', and the finale from Beethoven's 'Pastoral Symphony'; 'The Storm' was simply magnificent, and no orchestra could produce a more telling or effective tempest. The peculiarity, the oddity, of the performance, consisted in his playing the first eight bars of the 'Scherzo' rather quicker than they are usually taken, and the following eight bars, the D major phrase, in a slow andante time; 'ce sont les vieux', [these are the old people] he said to me on one occasion.[27]

Berlioz, in *Les Soirées de l'orchestre*, gives an account of Liszt's performance of the 'Emperor' Concerto at Bonn in 1845:

It would really be wasting words to say that Liszt. . . . played it in a grandiose, refined, poetic yet always faithful way. He received a blast of applause and orchestral fanfares that must have been audible even outside the hall. Afterwards, Liszt . . . conducted a performance of the C minor symphony, whose scherzo he let us hear just as Beethoven wrote it, without cutting the double-basses at the beginning . . . and with the repeat in the Finale as Beethoven indicated. . . .[28]

And Saint-Saëns, in his *Portraits et Souvenirs*, writes that Liszt

. . . never had the air of *a gentleman who plays the piano*. When he played *St. Francis de Paule Walking on the Waves* he looked like an apostle, and one thought one was seeing – one was really seeing – the foam of the furious waves flitting about his impassive and pale face, with its eagle-like look, its sharp profile. . . . The memory of having heard him is consolation for no longer being young![29]

One cannot help noticing that many of the remarks cited here have mentioned Liszt's appearance at the piano, referring to his 'look' as one of the key elements in the impact of his performances. Amy Fay, a young American pianist who attended Liszt's classes in Weimar in 1873, commented very perceptively on this subject:

Lizst knows well the influence he has on people, for he always fixes his eyes on some one of us when he plays, and I believe he tries to wring our hearts. When he plays a passage, and goes *pearling* down the keyboard, he often looks over at me and smiles, to see whether I am appreciating it. But I doubt if he feels any particular emotion himself. . . . He is simply hearing every tone, knowing exactly what effect he wishes to produce and how to do it. . . . He is practically two persons in one – the listener and the performer. But what immense self-command that implies![30]

This is a very important observation; and it concerns not just Liszt but performers in general. It is not possible to convey in a masterly way the structure, the sense, the emotions of a piece of music while being completely absorbed oneself in those abstractions and feelings: one would lose control of oneself and of the material at hand. Those discoveries and experiences belong for the most part to the period of preparation, when the performer comes to grips with the work; and it is only when the various elements have been completely assimilated – when, in fact, the performer has convinced himself that he has understood the terms dictated by the work itself – that he can hope to convince, and by convincing to move, his public. While in the act of performing he must listen to himself in as detached a way as possible, in order to reproduce his by now well-formed conception of the work as clearly as possible. Of course the excitement of communicating an interpretation, the tension of performing – these and other factors as well contribute their own emotion to a performance; and it would be absurd to imply that all performers feel nothing towards the music they play while they are playing it (although that may be the case with some). Nevertheless, the position of an outstanding pianist or violinist or singer is very similar to that of an outstanding actor who has given a great deal of thought to the meaning of a text, and who is therefore free, once before the public, to concentrate upon his delivery.

Liszt, obviously, was an outstanding performer and 'not a mere pianist', as Mendelssohn said. Mere pianist? To achieve Liszt's technical level would be quite a feat; and Mendelssohn, himself a pianist of fame, was well aware of that. What he meant was that Liszt, far from satisfying himself with technical accomplishments, however dazzling, also knew how to play with passion and imagination, how to create the most effective sort of atmosphere about himself and, in short, how to hold an audience in his grip. Moscheles's remark to the effect that Liszt always knew the public he was playing to is very revealing: when seated before a vast throng he could incite enthusiasm by throwing himself at the keyboard like a whirlwind; from a Hanslick or a George Eliot or a Saint-Saëns he could elicit descriptions of saints and apostles, gods and prophets; and he could overwhelm his students by smiling roguishly at them while performing horrifyingly difficult technical acrobatics – thus indicating his superiority to and detachment from his task. He knew how to suit the action not only to the word, but to whichever type of spectator – barren or otherwise – happened to be before him.

It is worthwhile to dip a bit deeper into Amy Fay's book for the insights it offers into both Liszt's musical ideas and his personality.

Liszt looks as if he had been through everything, and has a face *seamed* with experience. He is rather tall and narrow, and wears a long abbé's coat reaching nearly down to his feet. He made me think of an old time magician. . . . Liszt is just like a monarch, and no one dares speak to him until he addresses one first, which I think no fun.[31]

Yesterday I had prepared for him his *Au Bord d'une Source*. I was nervous and played badly. He was not to be put out, however, and acted as if he thought I had played charmingly, and then he sat down and played the whole piece himself, oh, *so* exquisitely! It made me feel like a woodchopper. The notes just seemed to ripple off his fingers' ends with scarce any perceptible motion. . . .[32]

[Student plays a Liszt concerto for Liszt] . . . in one place, where V. was playing the melody rather feebly, Liszt suddenly took his seat at the piano and said, 'When *I* play, I always play for the people in the gallery, so that those persons who pay only five groschen for their seat also hear something.' . . . The sound didn't seem to be very *loud*, but it was penetrating and far-reaching. . . .[33]

Fräulein Gaul was playing something to him, and in it were two runs, and after each run two staccato chords. She did them most beautifully, and struck the chords immediately after. 'No, no,' said Liszt, 'after you make a run you must wait a minute before you strike the chords, as if in admiration of your own performance. You must pause, as if to say, "How nicely I did that." ' Then he sat down and made a run himself, waited a second, and then struck the two chords in the treble, saying as he did so "Bra-*vo*", and then he played again, struck the other chord, and said again "Bra-*vo*", and positively it was as if the piano had applauded! That is the way he plays everything. It seems as if the piano were speaking with a *human* tongue.[34]

Fay ends her remarks on Liszt by comparing him with another of her musical heroes, the great violinist Joseph Joachim:

. . . Liszt, in addition to his marvellous playing, has this unique and imposing personality, whereas at first Joachim is not specially striking. Liszt's face is all a play of feature, a glow of fancy, a blaze of imagination, whereas Joachim is absorbed in his violin, and his face has only an expression of fine discrimination and of intense solicitude to produce his artistic effects. . . . Liszt is a complete actor who intends to carry away the public, who never forgets that he is before it, and who behaves accordingly. Joachim is totally oblivious of it. Liszt . . . said to us in the class one day, 'When you come out on the stage, look as if you didn't care a rap for the audience, and as if you knew more than any of them. That's the way I used to do. – Didn't that provoke the critics though!' he added, with an ineffable look of malicious mischief. So you see his principle. . . . Joachim, on the contrary, is the quiet gentleman-artist. . . . In reality I admire Joachim's principle the most, but there is something indescribably fascinating about Liszt's wilfulness. You feel at once that he is a great genius, and that *you* are nothing but his puppet, and somehow you take a base delight in the humiliation![34]

Another Liszt pupil, Emil Sauer, has also left a revealing account of the teaching and playing of Liszt in old age.

The master demanded a large degree of plasticity, clarity and purity of elocution and he attached the highest value possible towards having the pupil maintain a singing tone at the keyboard. In order to produce a beautiful sonority he wanted an artistic treatment of the pedal. He permitted the use of the una corda pedal only where there was a real necessity for doing so.[36]

Sauer says that while men, or women of no beauty, who played badly for Liszt were usually sent packing quickly, pretty young ladies could play on and on.

[Fräulein S.] bores us almost to death for half an hour, while the master, with a delighted smile, now and then letting his hand drop on her shoulder, helps her over false notes and rhythmic confusion and with an occasional 'Good!' tranquilly allows her to murder his piece . . .[37]

Sauer's descriptions of Liszt at the keyboard bear out most of the other testimony cited. He watched the old man playing his own arrangement of Paganini's *La campanella*:

He himself played it in tempo allegretto with an elegance, a lightness, and with indescribable charm. He took the great two-octave leaps generously, with head raised high and without fixing his glance upon the keys, while the bell struck its rhythms automatically. What a delightful, ennobled Campanella. . . .[38]

On one occasion, Liszt played for his students one of his own *Consolations*, Chopin's Nocturne in B-flat minor and Weber's *Perpetuum mobile*:

I was prepared for the fact that flexibility and elasticity of touch could not be expected from a septuagenarian, but not for the surprise of finding that his musical performance produced no impression to speak of upon me. What was truly remarkable, however, was the silent play of the eye, of face and feature, the classic pose of the entire person. All this revealed not a pianistic but a dramatic talent of the highest order.[39]

It would be wrong, however, to be excessively harsh on Liszt for this: many an aging artist has known that when all else fails, the Presence may still be enough; and others who heard Liszt in his last years have spoken quite differently of his playing. J. A. Fuller-Maitland was present at a party in the Grosvenor Gallery, London, during the pianist's last visit to England, just a few weeks before his death. Liszt was, as usual, successfully prevailed upon to play; and, reported Fuller-Maitland:

Notwithstanding his great age and his ill-health . . . one could realise the magic of his execution of those rapid passages in the higher parts of the piano, of which he was so very fond. It seemed to me that their extraordinary sparkle was got by keeping the fingers almost stiff, and letting the whole hand whip them off. . . .[40]

Of course a great deal was written about Liszt's technique by people who heard him in his prime. One example – of great potential interest to those familiar with keyboard technique in general – appeared in C. F. Weitzmann's book, *A History of Pianoforte-Playing and Pianoforte-Literature*, which was published not long after Liszt's death:

. . . Liszt did not hold his hand horizontally, but with the wrist higher than the front part. . . . If the fingers then rise to the height of the wrist, they gain all the more strength for the down-stroke upon the keys. Liszt sometimes played a more strongly-marked series of tones with the more powerful second finger alone, and a similar octave passage with the thumb and the third or fourth fingers; for a sustained or loud trill he used not only two adjoining fingers, but pairs separated by others, such as first and third, or third and fifth; the right hand executed such trills in suitable places even with the following fingering: 1–4 2–3, 1–4 2–3, etc. He likewise produced a sharp trill in sixths or thirds by playing the main notes with the right hand, and the subsidiary notes with the left, with equal power. For a passage regularly repeated in different octaves, he chose the most convenient fingering in *one* octave and repeated the same in the following octaves, when it frequently occurs, in opposition to earlier rules, that the thumb is passed under the fifth finger, or the latter over the thumb.[41]

Whether or not this description of Liszt's fingering is accurate, and whatever it was that he did to produce his effects, it is undeniable that no pianist has ever made as great or as lasting an impression as Liszt. Today, we divide the musical world into creators and performers; we prohibit tampering with the classics of musical literature; and we look upon improvisation with suspicion, keeping it in separate pigeonholes which we label either 'jazz' or, more forbiddingly, 'aleatoric music'. These restraints were much less stringent in Liszt's day, and he, for one, did not feel them at all. For him, performing and creating were a single dynamic entity. He himself wrote:

The virtuoso is not a mason who, chisel in hand, faithfully and conscientiously whittles stone after the design of an architect. He is not a passive tool reproducing feeling and thought and adding nothing of himself. . . . Spiritedly-written musical works are in reality, for the virtuoso, only the tragic and moving *mise-en-scène* for feelings. He is called upon to make emotion speak, and weep, and sing, and sigh – to bring it to life in his consciousness. He creates as the composer himself created, for he himself must live the passions he will call to light in all their brilliance. He breathes life into the lethargic body, infuses it with fire, enlivens it with the pulse of grace and charm. He changes the earthy form into a living being, penetrating it with the spark which Prometheus snatched from Jupiter's flesh. He must send the form he has created soaring into transparent ether: he must arm it with a thousand winged weapons; he must call up scent and blossom, and breathe the breath of life.[42]

Chapter Three

Anton Rubinstein

❖❖

'I play as a musician, not as a virtuoso.'

WITH THE EXCEPTION of Liszt, Anton Rubinstein was the most celebrated pianist of the nineteenth century; yet by most reports his taste, manner and mentality set him apart from nearly all his contemporaries in the field. He refused to accept the rôles of keyboard gymnast and romantic sorcerer and instead put his prodigious technique and intellectual powers to work in the service of music. The severe Eduard Hanslick wrote of him: 'It is a delight, in the highest and most sincere sense of the word, to listen to him. A vigorous and wholesome current of feeling flows so refreshingly over the hearer that he receives the impression of having been in a musical symposium, to the indescribable delectation of the ear.'[1] Another critic said: 'No artist has ever before shown to his audience so merciless a front. Both his programmes and his attitude are absolutely uncompromising. . . . Rubinstein has no idea of descending to the level of popular taste; he can only raise his audience to his own plane.'[2] And years after Rubinstein's death Rachmaninov stated: 'It was not so much his magnificent technique that held one spellbound as the profound, spiritually refined musicianship, which spoke from every note and every bar he played, and singled him out as the most original and unequalled pianist in the world.'[3]

These descriptions all deal with Rubinstein's playing during the 1880s, when he was in his fifties and at the height of his powers. Since he was then a master whose reputation and popularity were established beyond all doubt, he decided to attempt to illustrate in a bold way the entire development of keyboard music; and he brought the art of the performing musician to a new level of seriousness when, during the 1885–6 season, he gave a now legendary series of 'historical recitals' throughout Europe. He wrote that 'lectures on the history of music had been given before, but not historical concerts on the scale that I proposed.'[4]

His claims were valid; for it is safe to say that no other piano virtuoso of the nineteenth century had his wide-ranging knowledge of the entire keyboard repertoire – and certainly no other performing musician had the authority, desire and determination to present to his public such a challenging series of recitals. He prepared seven programmes of such mammoth proportions that one reads them with disbelief: each one lasted two or three times as long as a normal recital today. (Even the admiring Hanslick complained that Rubinstein's programmes were 'too much for even the strongest nerves.')[5]

The first recital began with the English virginalists Byrd and Bull (one piece each), proceeded to Couperin (six pieces) and Rameau (three), continued with Scarlatti (two), Bach (nine – including the Chromatic Fantasy and Fugue and excerpts from *The Well-Tempered Clavier*, among other pieces), Handel (five), Carl Philipp Emanuel Bach (five) and Haydn (the Variations in F minor), and ended with four works by Mozart, including a C minor Fantasy and the Rondo in A minor. The entire second programme was occupied by Beethoven sonatas – eight of them: the 'Moonlight', the 'Tempest', the 'Waldstein', the 'Appassionata', and Opp. 90, 101, 109 and 111! Recital No. 3 consisted of music by Schubert, Weber and Mendelssohn – twenty-one pieces, long and short. No. 4 was entirely devoted to Schumann and comprised the C Major *Fantasiestücke*, the *Vogel als Phophet*, the Romance in D minor and *Carnaval*. Sixteen pieces by Field, Moscheles, Henselt, Thalberg and Liszt made up the fifth programme, while thirty works of Chopin – including the F minor Fantasy, all four Ballades, the B minor Scherzo, B-flat minor Sonata, Barcarolle, Berceuse, and an assortment of préludes, mazurkas, impromptus, nocturnes, waltzes and polonaises – more than filled the sixth. The final programme began with eleven Chopin études and concluded with eight pieces by Rubinstein's compatriots and contemporaries: Glinka, Balakirev, Tchaikovsky and Rubinstein's brother Nicholas.

This entire series was performed in St Petersburg, Moscow, Vienna, Berlin, Leipzig, London and Paris; and, as Rubinstein tells us,

in some of them every concert that I gave in the evening was repeated the next day for the benefit of the music students. Both morning and evening concerts were crowded. . . . I played in St. Petersburg and Moscow alternately, giving two concerts in the one city and then two in the other, until fourteen concerts had been given in each. . . . Much of what I played at the concerts I had studied when I was a child. . . . As to the rest, I spent one summer in studying a good deal of the music that I now played for the first time.'[6]

The Times reported (14 June 1886) of his London series:

So great has been the success of Herr Rubinstein's historic piano recitals that the original series of seven had to be supplemented by an eighth concert, given on Friday last week before a vast audience. Of the educational task undertaken by the famous pianist, and of the manner in which he has carried it out with unflagging zeal, repeated mention has been made in *The Times*. Those of his audience who have travelled with him the long way from Couperin and Bach to Liszt and Tschaikovsky may say that the development of pianoforte music is no longer a sealed book to them. . . . It is by tracing this gradual growth through its various phases that Rubinstein has made his recitals so valuable to the student, displaying at the same time his own genius as an executant in the most brilliant light.

The historical recitals were the climax of Rubinstein's performing career. In them he achieved a fusion of virtuosity, musicianship and erudition unequalled by anyone before him and by few since. Moreover, those recitals were among the three achievements which assured Rubinstein of a special place in musical history. The other two were his fundamental work in founding the St Petersburg Conservatory, thereby preparing the way for Russia's emergence as a major musical power, and his discovery of America as a great gold mine for major European artists. So little information is available about Rubinstein today that it is important to provide some of the background to these and other of his accomplishments.

Anton Rubinstein was a successful mixture of seemingly incompatible elements. He was born on 16 November (Old Style; 28, New Style) 1829 in Vikhvatinyetz, a village on the Dnyestr river, about 150 kilometres north-west of Odessa, near what is today the border between the Moldavian and the Ukrainian Soviet Socialist Republics. His father, Gregori Romanovich Rubinstein, was a native of Berdichev, near Kiev; but his mother, Kaleria Christoforovna, *née* Levenstein, was from Prussian Silesia. When Anton, the third of six children, was not yet two, his paternal grandfather ordered the entire Rubinstein family, sixty in number, to convert from Judaism to Russian Orthodoxy in order to avoid the consequences of Tsar Nicholas

I's recently promulgated anti-Semitic ukase. So Anton, born a Jew, was brought up a Christian, at least nominally, in a household where three languages, Yiddish, Russian and German, were spoken. (In later years, when his musical 'Russianness' was called into question, he lamented: 'To the Jews I am a Christian, to the Christians a Jew; to the Russians a German, to the Germans a Russian; to the classicists a Wagnerite, to the Wagnerites a reactionary; and so on. Conclusion: I am neither fish nor flesh – a wretched individual!')[7]

One of the benefits of conversion was freedom of movement. Jews were not permitted to live in St Petersburg or Moscow, among other places; but the Rubinsteins could now go wherever their modest means permitted. In 1834 Gregori Romanovich moved his family to Moscow, where he opened a small pencil factory. The following year Anton's brother Nicholas was born; and he, like Anton, was to play an important part in Russian musical life.

Kaleria Rubinstein was a competent musician; and when Anton was five, she began to give him piano instruction. He later reported that the lessons were

not only serious, but often severe, in accordance with the method of teaching common in those days; but, as she afterwards admitted, she had never conceived any definite plan for my future musical career – teaching me simply because she was a musician herself. Our *repertoire* included Hummel, Herz, Moscheles, Kalkbrenner, Czerny, Diabelli, Clementi and other musical celebrities of those days. . . .[8]

The boy must have taken to the instrument amazingly well, because after a year-and-a-half Alexandre Villoing (1804–78), Moscow's leading piano teacher, heard him and accepted him as a non-paying student. Once again one must turn to Rubinstein's own words:

Villoing especially devoted much time and pains – with most successful results – to the correct position of my hands. He was most particular in this regard, as well as in the care he bestowed on the production of a good tone. . . . To him and to no one else am I indebted for a thorough, firm foundation in *technique* – a foundation which could never be shaken. [He was] a patient although strict master – the latter quality no less essential than the former. . . . In those days the method of teaching was very stern – ferules, punches and even slaps on the face were of frequent occurrence. . . .[9]

Anton gave his first public performance, a charity benefit concert, in the Petrovsky park, Moscow, on 11 July (O.S.) 1839, well before his tenth birthday. His programme consisted of music by some of the popular composers of the day: Hummel, Thalberg, Liszt, Field and Henselt. A Moscow daily, *Galatea*, noted: 'Music lovers have begged his parents to permit the sweet little artist to give at least one more concert, but the parents have declined this flattering request.'

Later that year Kaleria sent her son, accompanied by Villoing, to Paris to enrol at the Conservatoire. Cherubini, who was then, as in Liszt's day, director of that eminent institution, refused even to grant an audition to yet another of the child prodigies who were then plaguing Europe. In later years Rubinstein also suspected that Villoing, 'who regarded me as his own creation, was reluctant to part with me, or to entrust my musical education to anyone other than himself.'[10] For a year they remained in Paris, where Villoing sequestered his pupil and made him work at the piano many hours each day. Anton gave a few private performances, and finally, in December 1840, he played at the Salle Erard to an audience that included Chopin, Liszt and Meyerbeer. Chopin invited Anton to his studio, where he honoured the extraordinary child by playing him some of his mazurkas. Liszt acclaimed the young Rubinstein as his successor, but advised Villoing to take the boy to Germany for serious studies in composition. Villoing, however, overwhelmed by tempting requests for his protégé to perform all over Europe, arranged an extended tour that took them to Amsterdam, Vienna, Budapest, Berlin, London, Norway, Sweden, Warsaw and St Petersburg, among other places. In a letter of January 1841 Clara Schumann wrote to her friend Emilie List:

There is now an eleven-year-old boy in Vienna who is said to be the greatest genius to have been born in a long time; and we have learned this from people who are very hard to please. The boy is called Rubinstein and is a pianist; he is said to have a profound mind and in various areas a finished technique. . . . I should very much like to meet the boy – he is said to be a phenomenon.[11]

In London Rubinstein was received by the young Queen Victoria and played for Mendelssohn and Moscheles. The latter noted in his diary: 'This Russian boy has fingers light as feathers, and with them the strength of a man.'[12] A London critic, William Ayrton, left the following interesting description of the young pianist:

[He] excited the astonishment not only of those who are easily and willingly surprised by youthful genius. . . . This lad, who is small for his age and very slenderly made, though his head is of large dimensions – executes with his little hands the very same music in which Thalberg excels. . . . We . . . can answer for the unimpeachable correctness of his performance; and, what is still more remarkable, for the force by which, through some unparalleled gift of nature, he is enabled to exert a degree of muscular strength which his general conformation, and especially that of his arms and hands, would have induced us to suppose he could not possibly possess. To gratify those whose taste leads them to prefer fashionable music, he plays the fantasias of Liszt, Thalberg, Herz, etc.; but when exhibiting before real connoisseurs he chooses for his purpose the elaborate compositions of the old German school – the learned and difficult fugues of Sebastian Bach and Handel – all of which he executes with an ease as well as a precision which very few masters are able to attain; and, to add to the wonder, he plays everything from memory. . . .[13]

The travellers returned to Moscow in June 1843, after an absence of three-and-a-half years. Kaleria Rubinstein, who had spoken with Liszt during a concert tour he had recently made in Russia, was determined to follow his advice and to ensure a thorough grounding in musical theory for both Anton and Nicholas by taking them to Germany. To raise money for this project Anton and Villoing were dispatched on a tour of Russia. No sooner had the tour ended than Anton and Nicholas, aged fourteen and eight respectively, were sent to Petersburg by themselves to play for Tsar Nicholas and the imperial family at the Winter Palace. Finally, in the spring of 1844, the two boys, their mother and their sister Luba said goodbye to Gregori Romanovich and set out for Berlin.

There the Rubinsteins were warmly received both by Meyerbeer, who was then director of the Royal Opera and Court Orchestra, and by the Mendelssohn family. Mendelssohn said that Anton needed no further piano instruction but sent Nicholas to study with Theodor Kullak, while Meyerbeer directed both boys to Siegfried W. Dehn for harmony lessons. (Dehn had earlier taught another Russian – one whom Rubinstein would later consider to be a truly great composer: Mikhail Glinka.) A Greek Orthodox priest was engaged to instruct them in the catechism and in Russian grammar, and they studied other subjects as well. Although Rubinstein's formal non-musical studies were desultory and short-lived, he grew up to be a highly cultured, widely-read artist, perfectly fluent in Russian, German, French and English and capable of reading Italian and Spanish literature as well.

In the summer of 1846 word arrived that Gregori Romanovich was gravely ill. Leaving Anton in Berlin, Kaleria returned to Moscow with Nicholas and Luba, only to find her husband dead. His business had failed and he had left debts to be paid. Nicholas was sent on a concert tour to earn money, Kaleria found a job as a governess in a private school, and Anton had to survive on his own in Berlin. He continued his studies with Dehn and later with A. B. Marx and began to compose in earnest. Now seventeen years old, he could no longer pass as a child prodigy; and he decided to go to Vienna to ask Liszt for his help and protection. But, as he recounts in his autobiography, Liszt received him in a

cold and distant manner. He bade me remember that a talented man must win the goal of his ambition by his own unassisted efforts. This estranged me from him. I made several other calls, having brought with me some ten or fifteen letters of introduction from . . . the Russian Ambassador and his wife in Berlin. I made the calls and left the letters. . . . Silence was the sole response. . . . I was utterly at a loss. 'Let me look,' I thought, 'and see what is said about me in these letters of introduction', quite a pile of which still remained undelivered. I opened one of them, and what did I read! . . . 'My dear Countess So and So, To the position which we, the Ambassador and his wife, occupy, is attached the tedious duty of patronizing and recommending our various compatriots in order to satisfy their oftentimes clamorous requests. Therefore we recommend to you the bearer of this letter, one Rubinstein.' The riddle was solved. [14]

Rubinstein began giving piano lessons, spending as much time as possible producing compositions in every genre, and even writing literary, philosophic and critical essays. He often went without food for two or three days at a time. After two months Liszt remembered him and decided to pay him a visit.

He showed much tact and delicacy, and in the most friendly manner asked me to dine with him on the same day – a most welcome invitation. . . . After this I was always on good terms with Liszt until the time of his death. As for the music I wrote while in Vienna, but a small part of it appeared in print. . . . [15]

At the end of a year's residence in Vienna he gave a concert in the Bösendorfersaal; but the months of composing had reduced his piano practice time. He did not play well, and the venture was unsuccessful. Together with a flautist he went on a concert tour of Hungary, then returned to Berlin, where he resumed giving lessons. 'Some of the lessons were well paid, but as in Vienna, and afterwards in St Petersburg, I led the Bohemian life of an artist, feasting when money was plentiful and going hungry when it was gone. . . .'[16]

The revolution of 1848 put an end even to his restricted earning activities in Germany, and he returned to Russia. The next five years were spent mainly in St Petersburg where, apart from teaching and squandering his earnings, he gave concerts and performed frequently at the imperial court. The Grand Duchess Yelena Pavlovna, sister of Tsar Nicholas, was his most devoted patroness; and Rubinstein, despite his cynical views on monarchy, maintained the highest esteem for this 'truly remarkable woman. I never in my life met her equal.'[17] He credited her with great intelligence, human sympathy and dignity of manner, and claimed that she exercised a great reforming influence over her brother and later over her nephew, Alexander II, particularly on the controversial issue of the liberation of the serfs.

By 1852 Rubinstein had become a leading figure in St Petersburg's musical life. He performed not only as soloist, but also in partnership with some of the outstanding instrumental and vocal artists who were brought to the Russian capital, including the violinist Henri Vieuxtemps and the bass Luigi Lablache. Writing some years later, Vieuxtemps said of Rubinstein:

His power over the piano is something undreamt of; he transports you into another world; all that is mechanical in the instrument is forgotten. I am still under the influence of the all-embracing harmony, the scintillating passages and the thunder of Beethoven's Sonata Op. 57 ['Appassionata'], which Rubinstein executed for us with unimagined mastery.[18]

On occasion Rubinstein conducted the University Symphonic Concerts; and the première of his first opera, *Dmitri Donskoi*, on 18 April (O.S.) 1852, established his reputation as a serious composer. He often spent his summers as a guest of the Grand Duchess at her palace on Kammenoi-Ostrov (Stony Island), working at his compositions in a stimulating environment and free from economic worries. (One of his most popular piano pieces was in fact entitled *Kammenoi-Ostrov*.)

69

In 1854 Rubinstein undertook his first major concert tour in more than a decade. At twenty-four he now felt ready to appear before the public as a fully-developed pianist and as a composer of worth. One of his first stops was Weimar, where Liszt occupied the position of resident genius which had been held by Goethe earlier in the century. Rubinstein spent several long periods there that year, living at the Altenburg, Liszt's residence, and dining at the home of his host's companion, Princess Carolyne Sayn-Wittgenstein. Liszt, in a letter to his pupil Karl Klindworth, called Rubinstein

a clever fellow – the most notable musician, pianist and composer, indeed, who has appeared to me from among the newer lights, with the exception of the Murls [Liszt's disciples]. . . . But he possesses tremendous material, and an extraordinary versatility in the handling of it. He brought with him about forty or fifty manuscripts . . . which I read through with much interest. . . .[19]

To another student, Hans von Bülow, he wrote:

Do you know Rubinstein? He is a model worker and has an uncommon artistic individuality. . . . He is twenty-five [sic] years old, has true pianistic talent (which he has neglected in recent years); and it would be unjust to measure him by an ordinary yardstick.[20]

Some weeks later Liszt wrote to his friend Dr Franz Brendel, complimenting Rubinstein but referring to him as

the pseudo-Musician of the Future. . . . Still, I do not want to preach to him – he may sow his wild oats and fish deeper in the Mendelssohn waters, and even swim away if he likes. But sooner or later I am certain he will give up the apparent and the formalistic for the organically Real, if he does not want to stand still.[21]

Rubinstein and Liszt exchanged letters frequently during this period; but their correspondence deals almost entirely with composition. Between the two most celebrated pianists of the century there is barely a mention of piano technique. This was neither coincidence nor diplomatic tact. As we have already seen in Liszt's case, Rubinstein, too, clearly regarded himself primarily as a creative musician; performing was a far less important if much more profitable adjunct to his career.

His compositional output was vast: in addition to nineteen operas – the most popular of which was *The Demons* (1875) – he wrote choral works, six symphonies, symphonic poems, overtures, suites, concerti for piano, violin and cello, chamber music, sonatas for piano and for other instruments, miscellaneous piano music, songs etc. Many of his works achieved both public success and esteem within the profession. But while Liszt's compositions, although by no means universally admired, continue to hold a place in the repertoire and are even enjoying a certain resurgence of interest in our day, Rubinstein's have fallen into the most profound obscurity. Even Liszt's detractors will grant him his pioneering originality, while Rubinstein as a composer was purely an epigone – and, at that, an adherent of a school (Mendelssohn's, as Liszt rightly says) that was already considered conservative when Rubinstein was a boy.

Nevertheless, it was not long before he had re-established his reputation as a virtuoso. 'In power and execution he is inferior to no one', wrote Moscheles in 1855.[22] That opinion was now widespread; and with Liszt retired from the concert platform Rubinstein quickly became the most sought-after pianist of his generation. Saint-Saëns first heard him in Paris *circa* 1857 and later recalled, with characteristic hyperbole:

. . . from the first notes I was knocked down, harnessed to the conqueror's chariot! The concerts continued and I did not miss one of them.[23]

But Clara Schumann had reservations, and noted in her diary (London, 18 June 1857):

. . . Rubinstein visited me and played me several of his compositions, which interested me in part since they evidence much talent; however, I felt a lack of charm, which is also missing from his playing. He frightened me by his first hard attack on the piano, and then I didn't like his extemporizing at all: it seemed to me so unartistic to race all over the keyboard in thirds and sixths. . . . But his technique is very great all the same. We talked about Joachim and Johannes [Brahms]; he called them 'Priests of Virtue' – I don't believe that they go well together.[24]

A few days later Frau Schumann heard Rubinstein in concert and observed:

First he played Mendelssohn's Second Trio; but he rattled it about so horribly that I could barely sit still . . . and he oppressed the violin and cello so badly that I . . . often could not hear them. At the same time the piano often sounded awful, like glass, namely when he made his frightful tremolandos in the bass – truly ridiculous, but they delighted the public.[25]

71

Of these contrasting opinions, more later.

Rubinstein spent the winter of 1856–7 at Nice in Yelena Pavlovna's entourage. Much of the rest of the Russian imperial family was there as well, and Rubinstein jokingly gave himself the title 'Custodian of Music'. Those months on the Riviera were to have far-reaching consequences for Russia's musical life, for it was there that Rubinstein and members of the Grand Duchess's circle began to formulate plans for improving their country's system of musical education.

Although the Soviet Union today is officially and determinedly conservative in its musical outlook, no one would dream of calling it musically unproductive. Soviet-trained artists – those still based at home and those in exile in the West – dominate a surprisingly great proportion of international musical life. But a little over a century ago Russia was something of a musical desert. More than thirty years after his sojourn at Nice Rubinstein wrote:

. . . On one occasion, while I was performing my religious duties, I went to the confession in the Kazan Cathedral. [By Russian law every adult member of the Orthodox Church had to confess at least once every three years.] After confession I proceeded to the table to have my name enrolled in the books. The deacon began his enquiries. 'Your name, rank and vocation?' 'Rubinstein, artist,' I said. 'Are you employed in the theatre?' 'No,' 'Then perhaps you give lessions. . . ?' 'I do not,' I replied. The deacon appeared surprised, but no more so than I. . . . 'I am a musician, an artist,' I repeated. 'Yes, I understand; but are you in the government service?' 'I told you that I was not.' 'Who are you then? How shall we describe you?' . . . I know not how it would have ended had it not occurred to the deacon to say, 'May I ask your father's profession?' 'A merchant of the second guild.' 'Now, then, we understand!' exclaimed the deacon, greatly relieved. 'You are the son of a merchant of the second guild, and as such we shall inscribe your name.'[26]

The lowly position occupied by music and musicians in Russia bothered Rubinstein, and he determined to take upon himself fundamental responsibility for the transformation of the country's musical life. The Russian Musical Society was soon established in St Petersburg; and not long afterwards, at the Michael Palace, 'those classes were formed which may be regarded as the nucleus of the St Petersburg Conservatory'.[27] And what a faculty this fledgling group could boast of! Rubinstein was its director, Theodor Leschetizky professor of piano and Henri Wieniawski professor of violin, to name just three. 'In order to raise funds for the establishment, we used to give concerts nearly every day', wrote Rubinstein; and the excitement and competition were widespread. . . .'[28] The Conservatory itself was chartered in 1862, with Rubinstein as its director; and among its first class were Tchaikovsky, Annette Essipova (well-known pianist, later Leschetizky's wife and Prokofiev's teacher) and several others of outstanding talent. (In later years Rubinstein demonstrated no great love of Tchaikovsky's music; but he was personally kind to the younger composer. Tchaikovsky, to the end of his days, continued to revere Rubinstein.)

Before long Rubinstein and his Conservatory were attacked by 'The Five', that group of young composers – Balakirev, Borodin, Cui, Mussorgsky and Rimsky-Korsakov – who sought to give a non-academic and distinctly Russian flavour to their works. They opposed Rubinstein's pan-Europeanism and his professionalism. Balakirev was particularly rabid in his hatred of Rubinstein; Mussorgsky, the most gifted of the group, appears to have been more intimidated by Balakirev's attitude than truly preoccupied by the situation; while Rimsky-Korsakov, the most influential, eventually came to agree with Rubinstein in many respects. Rubinstein's attitude towards them was absolutely consistent with both his basic outlook and his personal generosity: he rejected their philosophy but played and conducted those of their works which he judged worthwhile. In the 1860s the dispute was particularly frenzied; and to understand the resentment of 'The Five' one must remember that at that time and for a generation thereafter Rubinstein's music was far more popular than their own.

This and related matters created such dissension within the Conservatory's faculty that Rubinstein angrily resigned in 1867. His concert activities, which had been reduced during his years as an administrator, were now resumed with great intensity. In London in 1868 he played Beethoven's 'Archduke' Trio with violinist Leopold Auer and cellist Alfredo Piatti. Auer has left his impressions of the pianist:

It was the first time I had heard this great artist play. He was most amiable at the rehearsal. . . . To this day I can recall how Rubinstein sat down at the piano, his leonine head thrown slightly back, and began the five opening measures of the principal theme. . . . It seemed to me I had never before heard the piano really played. The grandeur of style with

73

which Rubinstein presented those five measures, the beauty of tone his softness of touch secured, the art with which he manipulated the pedal, are indescribable. . . . Very simple in his manner, without any affectation of importance, he was charming in his relations with all artists, and, indeed, with all whom he regarded as devoted to the true cause of music.[29]

But Clara Schumann heard him in Breslau (now Wrocław) that same year and wrote in her diary: 'I was beside myself, because this was no longer playing; it was either a nonsensical pounding or an inaudible whisper. . . .'[30]

In 1869 Rubinstein was ennobled by the Tsar, who decorated him with the Vladimir Order; and for one season (1871–2) he assumed the directorship of Vienna's famed Gesellschaft der Musikfreunde (Friends of Music Society).

Then, at the end of August 1872, Rubinstein sailed from Liverpool towards New York for what was surely one of the most gruelling tours ever undertaken: an eight-month marathon that was to take him to more than sixty North American cities and towns. 'The things that happen to a musician!' he lamented years afterwards. His cabin on the outbound ship was near the motor.

Bedridden for the most part, since I take badly to sea voyages, I turned my attention by chance to the monotony of the motor's rhythm. The fatal thought occurred to me that the rhythm ought to change – something different, if only for a moment. . . . No and again no. The trip lasted ten days, and so did the unvarying rhythm. I was in unspeakable agony; I thought I'd gone mad; I broke into a cold sweat. When we finally arrived, the release from this torture was such bliss for me that I actually . . . greeted the New World with praise unto Heaven and with the thankfulness of one redeemed, delivered![31]

The tour was guaranteed by the Steinway Piano Company of New York and was managed by a young Czech emigrant, Maurice Grau, who was later to manage the Metropolitan Opera and then the Royal Opera, Covent Garden. While some sense of adventure may have helped to stir Rubinstein's interest in the project, there can be no doubt that the unheard-of fee of $200 per concert, with all expenses paid, was the principal attraction; for if he considered Russia a musical backwater, the United States must have appeared positively lunar to him. The Americans certainly regarded him as a sort of interplanetary visitor. He was the greatest pianist – in fact, the most famous musician – yet to have visited their country: a rare bird indeed. *The New York Times*, 13 September 1872:

The Philharmonic Society of New-York gave their first serenade last night since the one they accorded to Jenny Lind. The recipient of this distinguished honor was Anton Rubinstein, the pianist, who recently arrived in this City. The desire to see Rubinstein, joined to the exquisite harmonies of the Philharmonic orchestra, attracted a large concourse of people around the Clarendon Hotel, and between the morceaux loud cheers and calls were given for Rubinstein. . . . Mr Strong [president of the Philharmonic Society] welcomed Rubinstein to America, to which Rubinstein replied in a few words of gratitude, uttered in excellent English. Loud calls being made for the pianist by the crowd in the street, he stepped out on the balcony and said: 'Gentlemen: I cannot find words to express my feelings or the gratitude that overpowers me; but I do assure you that I am deeply sensible of the honor you have conferred upon me, and the recollection of it will be one of the happiest of my life.' He then retired.

His first concert took place at Steinway Hall, New York, on 23 September, and included one of his own concerti, a piece by Handel, Mozart's Rondo in A minor, a march from Beethoven's *The Ruins of Athens* (arranged for piano) and Schumann's Symphonic Etudes. Wieniawski, who accompanied him throughout most of the tour as an assisting artist, also performed. The concert was of course an enormous success – and so was the rest of the tour. In New York alone Rubinstein performed in fifty concerts; twenty were given in Boston, twelve in Philadelphia, eleven in Chicago, ten in New Orleans, nine in Cincinnati, seven in Brooklyn, six each in St Louis and Washington, five in Baltimore, four each in Pittsburgh and Cleveland, three each in Newark, Albany, Hartford, Buffalo and Detroit, and one or two in each of forty-four other towns. By the time Rubinstein left for Europe he had given 216 scheduled concerts (plus extra performances) in approximately 245 days; the gross box office proceeds amounted to $350,000, and the pianist, as he boarded the *S.S. Donau* on 24 May 1873, carried with him his share of the earnings – the incredible sum of $46,000 in gold. In his memoirs Rubinstein wrote:

The receipts and the success were invariably gratifying, but it was all so tedious that I began to despise myself and my art. So profound was my dissatisfaction that when several years later I was asked to repeat my American tour, with half a million [francs] guaranteed to me, I refused point blank. . . . Under these conditions there is no chance for art – one grows into an automaton, simply performing mechanical work; no dignity remains to the artist, he is lost. [32]

The tour produced one famous piece of literary 'Americana' – a monologue entitled *How Ruby Played*, supposedly by a Texan named Joe Brownin; and I reproduce parts of it here because it is more entertaining and not less informative than most of the concert reviews from the tour.

When he first sit down, Rubin 'peared to keer mighty little 'bout playin', and wisht he hadn't come. He tweedle-leeded a little on the treble, and twoodle-oodled some on the bass – just foolin' and boxin' the thing's jaws for bein' in his way. . . . I was just about to git up and go home, bein' tired of that kind of foolishness, when I heard a little bird waking up away off in the woods, and call sleepy-like to his mate, and I looked up and see that Rubin was beginning to take some interest in his business. . . . Next thing it was broad day and the whole world as bright and happy as a king. . . . And I says to my neighbor: 'That's music, that is.'

Presently the wind turned; it began to thicken up, and a kind of gray mist came over things; I got low-spirited directly. . . . All of a sudden, old Rubin changed his tune. He ripped out and he rared, he tipped and he tared, he pranced and he charged like the grand entry at a circus. 'Peared to me that all the gas in the house was turned on at once, things got so bright. . . . He set every livin' joint in me a-goin', and not bein' able to stand it no longer, I jumped spang onto my seat, and jest hollered: 'Go it, my Rube!'

. . . I tell you the audience cheered. Rubin, he kinder bowed, like he wanted to say, 'Much obleeged, but I'd rather you wouldn' interrupt me.' He stopt a moment or two to ketch breath. Then he got mad. He run his fingers through his hair, he shoved up his sleeves, he opened his coattails a leetle further, he drug up his stool, he leaned over, and sir, he just went for that old pianner. He slapped her face, he boxed her jaws, he pulled her nose. . . . He knockt her down and he stampt on her shameful. . . .

Bang! He lifted himself bodily into the a'r and he come down with his knees, his ten fingers, his ten toes, his elbows, and his nose, striking every single solitary key on the pianner at the same time. The thing busted and went off into seventeen hundred and fifty-seven thousand five hundred and forty-two hemi-demi-semi-quivers, and I knowed no mo'.[33]

Rubinstein's earnings from his American tour gave him financial security for the rest of his life. He had married in 1865 (his wife's name was Vera Tchekuanov); and the couple had had three children – Jacob, Anna and Alexander. Now he was able to build a lovely *dacha* at Peterhof, not far from St Petersburg. His wife rarely accompanied him on his tours, and it appears that his marriage was not a happy one; but he always returned to Peterhof with pleasure. There he was able to compose and study in peace, and to entertain friends and colleagues. During the summer months he would often play chamber music with Auer and cellist Carl Davidoff; and great numbers of people would sit on the lawn and listen.

Clara Schumann saw Rubinstein in Vienna in 1885 and made the following notes in her diary:

Rubinstein very lively, but he is not a happy man; I think in fact that he feels that he has not reached the highest artistic summit. . . . The poor fellow! I can't look at him without feeling the deepest sympathy. . . . Rubinstein played Beethoven's G Major Concerto dreadfully (at the Museum). . . . He was received enthusiastically despite everything because he is greatly loved as a man. How celebrated Brahms would be if he had something of Rubinstein's lovableness. . . .[34]

The principal cities of Europe continued to welcome him regularly; but in his autobiography, published when he was nearly sixty, he admitted that he was having problems with his memory.

My musical memory . . ., until my fiftieth year, was prodigious; but since then, I have been conscious of a growing weakness. I begin to feel an uncertainty; something like a nervous dread often takes possession of me while I am on stage. . . . I often fear lest memory betray me into forgetfulness of a passage, and that I may unconsciously change it. . . . This sense of uncertainty has often inflicted upon me tortures only to be compared with those of the Inquisition, while the public listening to me imagines that I am perfectly calm.[35]

His health, too, was beginning to deteriorate: he suffered from shortness of breath and chest pains – a condition that he called asthma but that was in fact heart disease. Twice during his historical recital series in Paris he had had fainting spells; and although one of his St Petersburg friends and card partners was a physician, Rubinstein refused to be examined or to listen to advice that he moderate his smoking. (He was addicted to cigarettes.) On top of this, the death of his brother Nicholas in 1881 at the age of forty-six continued to depress him. Nicholas had himself founded the Moscow Conservatory and had been a great inspiration to young Russian musicians.

In 1887 Rubinstein resumed the directorship of the St Petersburg Conservatory, which he had abandoned twenty years earlier. It was his objective to improve the institution's standards by removing inferior students and raising the calibre of the faculty. He seems to have ruled as an autocrat, firing and demoting many professors, making entrance and examination requirements more stringent and revising the courses. He personally took the piano faculty in hand, leading a semi-weekly teachers' class through the whole keyboard literature. To some of the more gifted piano students he gave personal instruction – coaching, perhaps, would be a better term for it, since he wasn't interested in working on the mechanics of technique with them. He wanted to make them think about the music they were playing, about suiting the tone to the piece, the phrase; and his manner with them was a mixture of raw, sometimes violent, criticism and good humour. During the 1889–90 academic year he gave weekly lecture-recitals for the students.

Greetings and good wishes arrived from many parts of the world for Rubinstein's sixtieth birthday and the fiftieth anniversary of his first public appearance, both of which were celebrated in 1889. But his relations with the imperial family were on the decline. His old patroness Yelena Pavlovna had died many years earlier, and her grand-nephew Alexander III had not inherited the cultural interests of his father or grandfather. That year the Tsar made a perfunctory gesture towards Petersburg's musical life by donating the dilapidated old Bolshoi Theatre to the Conservatory as a site for the latter's new home; but he failed to endow it with the funds required to restructure and restore it. At a reception given in the Tsar's honour, the monarch asked Rubinstein whether he was pleased with the gift. With his customary bluntness, and to the horror of the other guests, the pianist replied: 'Your Imperial Majesty, if I gave you a beautiful cannon, all mounted and embossed, with no ammunition, would you like it?'[36]

Worse was to follow. Alexander III had previously restricted the number of Jews admitted to the Conservatory and to other institutions of higher education outside the Pale of Settlement to 3 per cent of the total student body (10 per cent at universities within the Pale). In 1891 he decided that Jews were winning too high a percentage of the Conservatory's annual prizes. These, too, he insisted, would be awarded in the future on the basis of the same racial quotas. Angered and disgusted, Rubinstein resigned the directorship of the Conservatory which he himself had conceived and founded nearly thirty years earlier, and which he considered to be the most important of his achievements.

Not many months earlier, shortly before his anniversary celebrations, he had written to Bartholf Senff, his Leipzig publisher:

I confess that the net result of all my artistic activity is the most complete disappointment. That upon which I have lavished all my hopes and all my study – my composition – is a failure. My whole existence is a mockery. I who am convinced that art is entirely dead, that no eight measures worth a penny are written nowadays, that even performing art – vocal and instrumental – is not fit to latch the shoestring of what has gone before – I, who believe this, spend my whole time educating pupils in composition and execution, knowing all the while that my efforts are love's labour lost. You can imagine, therefore, the irony I shall have to summon on the occasion of my so-called Jubilee this autumn. 'Eitel, eitel ist des Menschen.' [Vain, vain are all things human.] . . .[37]

Now his artistic disillusionment was compounded by his rage at the course of events in his native country. In despair, Russia's most famous musician left his homeland in September 1891 and went to live in Dresden. He began to give concerts again in Germany and Austria – almost entirely charity benefit events; and he composed and even coached a few exceptionally gifted piano students, including Josef Hofmann and Josef Lhévinne. Hofmann, then fifteen, later recalled:

Once I played a Liszt rhapsody pretty badly. After a little of it, Rubinstein said, 'The way you play this piece would be all right for Auntie or Mamma.' Then rising and coming toward me, he said, 'Now let us see how we play such things.'

I began again, but I had not played more than a few measures when Rubinstein said loudly, 'Have you begun?' 'Yes, Master, I certainly have.' 'Oh,' said Rubinstein vaguely, 'I didn't notice.' . . .

Rubinstein did not so much instruct me. Merely he let me learn from him. . . . If a student, by his own study and mental force, reached the desired point which the musician's wizardry had made him see, he gained reliance in his own strength, knowing he would always find that point again even though he should lose his way once or twice, as everyone with an honest aspiration is liable to do.[38]

Just as Rubinstein had been shaken by his brother Nicholas's premature death ten years earlier, so he was now greatly affected by the deaths first of his mother at the age of eighty-six – just a few days after her son's departure for Dresden – and then of his youngest son, Alexander, who succumbed to tuberculosis two years later at the age of twenty. Rubinstein returned periodically to Russia to visit family and friends; and then, aware that his health was failing rapidly, he moved back to Peterhof in the summer of 1894. There he died on 8 (20, N.S.) November, a few days before his sixty-fifth birthday. Clara Schumann noted in her diary that same day:

News of Rubinstein's sudden death. . . . Great demonstrations of sympathy everywhere, and there will be no lack of musical commemorations; but how will things go afterwards? Won't all his operating, all his undertakings in favour of his compositions, disappear? It is sad to think of it; poor man – governed by such restless ambition.[39]

Although descriptions of Rubinstein's playing differ in many respects, one can draw certain general conclusions from them. At its best, it was of a compelling, poetic quality – that rare sort of music-making which can only occur when the performer has both an intense inner conviction about the music he is playing and the technical ability to realize, or at least to come near to realizing, his own vision. On the other hand, there were times when he seemed to lose control of his own temperament and to play in an almost incoherently rhapsodic, even brutal manner. A review in *The Times*, London, 8 June 1877, describes some of Rubinstein's excesses, after praising his performances of the Mozart Rondo in A minor and other pieces:

Nothing can be more simple, unobtrusive, and poetically beautiful than his delivery of these. . . . He shines with a special grace, producing a tone from the instrument, combined with the most admirably perfect phrasing, which shows him to be a singer by natural instinct. His method of dealing with Beethoven is less unreservedly to be commended. . . . ['Appassionata' Sonata:] Nothing can be more perfect than the way in which he gives the *andante* with variations . . . while the whole of the *finale*, which though marked by the composer simply 'allegro non troppo' . . . is taken by Herr Rubinstein at such a pace that when the *coda*, marked 'presto', comes, it is little better than confusion. . . . In Liszt's monstrous 'transcription' of the 'Erl-King', . . . Herr Rubinstein was quite at home; but in Schumann's 'Carnaval' we found too much display at the expense of the composer. . . . [A Chopin polonaise:] Why, for example, the hands of the pianist should be lifted above his head, only to fall down upon a succession of chords that any schoolgirl might strike without moving her fingers from the keyboard, escapes our comprehension. . . . To us it seems nothing but superfluous gesticulation, unworthy of one gifted with such wonderful mechanical powers as Herr Rubinstein possesses. . . .

Seven years later, Hanslick reviewed a series of Rubinstein concerts in Vienna and expressed similar opinions in a more understanding way:

To hear Rubinstein play is pleasure in the finest sense of the word. . . . His healthy, robust sensuality floods upon the listener with refreshing candour. His virtues are rooted in his unsapped natural strength and elemental freshness. So also are the faults into which his rich, but frequently unbridled, headstrong talent easily tempts him. Compared with former years, his playing is a model of refinement. The melting beauty of his tone, the softness and concentrated strength of his touch, are at the very peak. . . . No one can sing more beautifully than Rubinstein played in his performance of Beethoven's Sonata in D minor. In Schumann's Sonata in F-sharp minor the slow movement was ideally beautiful. . . . The Finale, on the other hand, was overwhelmed in such a manner that even listeners thoroughly familiar with it were not always able to keep pace and were often left to guess what he had actually played. He did Chopin's Barcarolle with charming delicacy, and then whipped through the C-sharp minor Polonaise, Opus 26, in such a manner that the elegant charm of the piece, and sometimes even its rhythmic pattern, fell breathless by the wayside. Even Schumann's Fantasy in C major, which he began wonderfully, was rendered disorderly and blustery by the exaggeration of the E-flat major middle section. That Rubinstein exerts his fascination even in such moments as these is probably because the audience senses that his excesses derive from an irresistible primeval force rather than from mere vanity of virtuosity. [40]

Rachmaninov was a thirteen-year-old student at the Moscow Conservatory when Rubinstein gave his historical recitals there, and he heard each programme twice. Some of his general impressions were cited at the very beginning of this chapter; the more specific ones are also valuable:

Once he repeated the whole finale of [Chopin's] Sonata in B minor, perhaps because he had not succeeded in the short crescendo at the end as he would have wished. One listened entranced, and could have heard the passage over and over again, so unique was the beauty of tone. . . . I have never heard the virtuoso piece *Islamey* by Balakirev, as Rubinstein played it, and his interpretation of Schumann's little fantasy *The Bird as*

Prophet was inimitable in poetic refinement: to describe the diminuendo of the pianissimo at the end as the 'fluttering away of the little bird' would be hopelessly inadequate. Inimitable, too, was the soul-stirring imagery in the *Kreisleriana*, the last (G minor) passage of which I have never heard anyone play in the same manner. One of Rubinstein's greatest secrets was his use of the pedal. He himself very happily expressed his ideas on the subject when he said: 'The pedal is the soul of the piano.' No pianist should ever forget this.[41]

A few years later Rachmaninov heard Rubinstein accompanying a singer, Mme Lavrovskaya (one of his former lovers), in two of his own songs.

I noticed that he did not keep strictly to the music before him, but seemed at times to improvise, illustrating the two rather weak compositions . . . with such striking flashes of tone colour that one was unable ever to forget them again.[42]

Rachmaninov admitted that Rubinstein's playing was not always perfectly accurate, but said that 'for every possible mistake he may have made, he gave, in return, ideas and musical tone pictures that would have made up for a million mistakes.'[43] Rubinstein himself, after a concert in Berlin in 1875, told Enole Mendelssohn: 'If I could gather up all the notes that I let fall under the piano, I could give a second concert with them.'[44]

Bernard Shaw admired Rubinstein's mastery of the keyboard but questioned his musical intentions. Commenting on Sir Charles Hallé's ability to draw an audience every time he played Beethoven sonatas, he asked:

Is there any audience in the world that would come to hear Rubinstein play a Beethoven sonata for the twentieth time? . . . The secret is that [Hallé] gives you as little as possible of Hallé and as much as possible of Beethoven, of whom people do not easily tire. When Beethoven is made a mere *cheval de bataille* for a Rubinstein, the interest is more volatile. The 'classical' players have the best of it in the long run.[45]

Rachmaninov, Hanslick, Hofmann, Lhévinne and an army of others would have contended this point with Shaw. They would have granted that Rubinstein's approach was highly personal, but would have insisted that his aim was purely to serve the music he played and not to use it for exhibitionistic purposes. However, J. A. Fuller-Maitland wrote:

In Rubinstein, nothing struck me so much as the exquisite simplicity with which the variations at the end of Handel's D minor Suite were played. In other things there was of course no lack of tones that were not always beautiful. . . . Rubinstein's Beethoven was presented in flashes of lightning, in sharp contrast with the clear and logical expositions of Hallé or the spasmodic and often dry interpretations of Bülow. . . . Rubinstein dealt mainly in extremes, but possessed perhaps as many as five or six different degrees of force, while Mme Schumann . . . revealed gradations that were impossible to number. . . .[46]

The American writer James Huneker heard the historical recitals in Paris and was as deeply impressed as Rachmaninov. But he reported that Georges Mathias and other pupils of Chopin had criticized Rubinstein as 'brutal in his treatment of their master'.[47]

In regard to keyboard technique and comportment Rubinstein himself tells us that as a young man he was 'a devoted imitator of Liszt, of his manners and movements, his trick of tossing back his hair, his way of holding his hands, of all the peculiar movements of his playing. . .'[48] Villoing had worked with him on hand position and finger dexterity; by watching Liszt, Rubinstein learned about freedom of arm movement. Ludwig Deppe, the German piano teacher, talked to the American pianist Amy Fay about Rubinstein:

He told me if I ever heard Rubinstein play again to observe how he strikes his chords. 'Nothing cramped about *him*! He spreads his hands as if he were going to take in the universe, and takes them up with the greatest freedom and *abandon*!' Deppe has the greatest admiration for Rubinstein's *tone*, which he says is unequalled, but he places Tausig above him as an artist.[49]

Leschetizky, who likened muscular relaxation at the piano to a singer's deep breathing, would remark to his students about 'what deep breaths Rubinstein used to take at the beginning of long phrases, and also what repose he had and what dramatic pauses.' Lhévinne said that Rubinstein had 'a fat, pudgy hand, with fingers so broad at the finger-tips that he often had difficulty in not striking two notes at one time'[50] – thus explaining at least some of Rubinstein's wrong notes. Finally, we have Proust's remark in *A l'ombre des jeunes filles en fleurs* about the grandmother who loved all that was natural in life – 'Rubinstein's mistakes, for example'.

❖❖❖

Rubinstein's physical appearance was unusual. 'It is very easy to describe me,' he told Lillian MacArthur, his Irish piano student and secretary. 'I am simply much hair and little nose.'[51] He was of medium height and slender build. Photographs show a large head, long, thick hair and a broad, squarish face. 'A felicitous combination of the German, the Sclave and the Semite' is how George Eliot described Herr Klesmer in *Daniel Deronda*. Klesmer was based on Rubinstein, whom the authoress had met at Liszt's in Weimar in 1854 and again in London in 1876 when she was completing her last novel. Rubinstein's eyes were blue and somewhat slanted, almost Tartarish, his forehead very high, and there were, said MacArthur, 'lines of passion and impetuosity about the mouth. . . . He bears a striking resemblance to Beethoven, and in a beautifully finished oil-painting of Augener in Vienna, taken when he was quite a young man, one might easily mistake him for the great Bonn master.'[52] (Moscheles, who knew both men, was also reminded of Beethoven by Rubinstein's features and hair, and Liszt called his younger colleague 'Van II'. Absurd rumours persisted throughout Rubinstein's life to the effect that he was Beethoven's illegitimate son – absurd because Beethoven died more than two-and-a-half years before Rubinstein was born.)

His writings and the impressions left us by others reveal an essentially unhappy man who yet managed to maintain a ready sense of humour. He liked his privacy; and in that epoch, when touring artists often spent weeks or even months, rather than hours, in the major towns on their itineraries, he would generally rent an entire house for himself in order to avoid public curiosity 'and the piano playing of English ladies'.[53] Stubbornly honest and not given to compromise, he was also generous and hospitable. 'I delight in his sincerity and simplicity,' wrote Moscheles; 'he is always a welcome visitor at our house.' Rubinstein seems to have been both greatly attracted and attractive to women.

A pantheist, he enjoyed mocking revealed religions. He told MacArthur that there are two classes of priests: 'those who deceive themselves and those who deceive others.'[55] Some of his thoughts on life and art, written down at random in his later years, were published posthumously in a German book entitled *Anton Rubinsteins Gedankenkorb* (*Anton Rubinstein's Thought-Basket*); but much more revealing and interesting is another book, *Music and Its Masters,* which was published in several languages within Rubinstein's lifetime. It takes the form of an extended conversation between the great musician and Mme de ———. Like the *Thought-Basket,* it dates from his last years. He begins by telling his friendly interrogator that for him, the five greatest composers are Bach, Beethoven, Schubert, Chopin and Glinka. Mozart is great, but not as great as the others. He then goes on to make an extraordinary statement, coming as it does from the composer of nineteen operas:

To me the opera is altogether a subordinate branch of our art. . . . The human voice sets a limit to melody, which the instrument does not, and of which the emotion of the human soul does not admit. . . . To me, for instance, the *Leonore* Overture No. 3 and the Introduction to the second act of *Fidelio* are a much higher expression of this drama than the opera itself. . . . To see gods, kings, priests, heroes, peasants. . . . act and sing to one's melody, has something very enticing in it; the highest, however, remains *to express oneself about them* – and that can be done instrumentally only. . . .

I hold that music is a language – to be sure, of a hieroglyphic, tone-image character; one must first have deciphered the hieroglyphics; then, however, one may read all that the composer intended to say, and there remains only the commentary. . . . [Of Chopin's Second Ballade:] Is it possible that the interpreter does not feel the necessity of representing to his hearer a field-flower caught by a gust of wind, a caressing of the flower by the wind; the resistance of the flower, the stormy struggle of the wind; the entreaty of the flower, which at last lies broken; or paraphrased, the field flower a rustic maiden, the wind a knight. . . ? I am for the programme which has to be *divined* and *devised,* not for the *given* programme of a composition. . . .

This idea of the visual image as a necessary aid to the performing artist was not uncommon among musicians of Rubinstein's time; and one comes upon it even today on occasion. But there is an obvious discrepancy in Rubinstein's reasoning: he has declared instrumental music to be superior to vocal music precisely because it is more abstract, because it exists in a region where words and other earthbound encumbrances do not weigh it down; he then presents the case for interpreting 'pure' music by providing it with a new set of encumbrances – and very arbitrary ones at that: they are much more likely to be misleading than words which, in the best of cases, have been skilfully married to the music of a vocal work.

85

Rubinstein's comments on the history of music are original and, for their day, of extraordinarily wide compass. He discusses Palestrina, Frescobaldi, Bull, Byrd, Scarlatti, Couperin, Rameau and Purcell as well as the later composers with whom one would expect him to have been familiar. He expresses the very conservative opinion that 'with the death of Schumann and Chopin "*finis musicae*"!' However, he considered Berlioz, Wagner and Liszt to be the most important composers of his day and called Berlioz the most interesting among the three.

Regarding interpretation, he begins by insisting that musicians must play from original-text editions of the classics and not from such standard nineteenth-century editions as Czerny's revision of *The Well-Tempered Clavier* or von Bülow's of the Beethoven sonatas. And he proceeds with some highly interesting comments:

The interpreter of today (conductor and virtuoso) delights especially in a capricious interpretation of the classical works (for which both Wagner and Liszt are most to blame) – change of tempo, pauses, ritardandos, stringendos, crescendos, etc., not written by the composer. . . . [On eliminating repeated passages:] It is really astounding that professional musicians can give themselves to such an unmusical proceeding! . . . Cutting . . . belongs to the same category of crime. . . . I am wholly at a loss to understand what is meant by the *objective* in interpretation. . . . Every interpretation, if it is made by a person and not by a machine, is *eo ipso, subjective*. To do justice to the *object* (the composition) is the law and duty of every interpreter; but of course each one in his own way, *i.e..*, subjectively. And how is any other way imaginable? . . . Of course, if a subjective interpretation makes an allegro of an adagio, or a funeral march of a scherzo, it becomes nonsense; but to render an adagio in a given tempo, according to one's own feeling, cannot be called doing injustice to the object.

The most remarkable aspect of Rubinstein's observations in *Music and Its Masters* is its demonstration of the high level of his musical conscientiousness and general artistic awareness. These are uncommon qualities in virtuosi of any era; in Rubinstein's time they were extraordinary. And however astonished we may be by his conservatism, it is nonetheless moving to think of him, at the end of a lifetime dedicated to playing, teaching and creating music, concluding his book with these words:

I feel that I shall not live long enough now to enjoy the coming Bach or Beethoven, and that is sorrowful to me. My only solace is that I may still have the same enthusiasm for an organ prelude or fugue of the Bach that was; for a sonata, a string quartet or a symphony of the Beethoven that was. . . . After having accompanied Mme de —— to her carriage, I returned to my studio, and remained standing there, meditating whether it may not be the *musical Götterdämmerung* that is now breaking upon us.[56]

Chapter Four

Ignace Jan Paderewski

❖❖❖❖❖❖❖❖❖❖❖❖❖❖❖❖❖❖❖❖❖❖❖❖❖❖❖❖❖❖❖❖❖❖❖

THE PADEREWSKI STORY is in one way even more extraordinary than the three preceding ones; for while Paganini, Liszt and Rubinstein were trained for their careers from childhood and were all seasoned concert artists by the time they reached their early teens, Paderewski received little useful instruction at the piano until adolescence and did not establish himself until he was nearly thirty. There were deficiencies in his technique which even the most assiduous practice never eliminated; yet he became the most celebrated instrumentalist of his generation, maintaining for decades the admiration of great numbers of musicians as well as that of the general public.

From the outset of his career it was clear that he was not to be just another fine key-pusher: he was a musician of insight, a man of wide culture, and a magnetic presence. 'Paderewski', said Saint-Saëns, 'is a genius who also happens to play the piano'; but this witticism does not offer a great deal of help in explaining the impression that Paderewski made upon his contemporaries. For that one must begin with an interesting passage in the memoirs of the famous Polish actress Helena Modjeska, who first heard Paderewski play when he was twenty-three, several years before his professional debut:

Paderewski's head, with its aureole of profuse golden hair and delicate, almost feminine features, looked like one of Botticelli's or Fra Angelico's angels, and he seemed so deeply wrapped up in his muse that this intensity was almost hypnotic. . . . We had many chats and I advised him to appear in public. His poetic face, combined with his genius, was bound to produce brilliant results.[1]

Modjeska instinctively saw Paderewski's potential as a stage personality; and Paderewski himself, within a few years, had learned how to combine what he himself called the effect of his personality with his exceptional musical instincts and his some-times dazzling, sometimes inadequate pianistic abilities. He was attentive to the cut of his clothes, to his great crown of

89

reddish-gold hair – a source of endless comment in the American press – and to his delicate moustache and tuft of underlip hair. He took care to prepare the atmosphere of his concerts by making his audiences wait a bit (and often more than a bit), by insisting that the house lights be down and the stage lights dim and by making slow, deep, dignified bows to the public. Travelling in his own elaborately furnished railway carriage, he had his own pianos and custom-made piano chairs hauled from town to town; and these seemingly extravagant practices attracted much attention. But he also thought a great deal about the music he played and worked very hard at preparing his interpretations.

In short, Paderewski offered something for nearly everyone, which is why the foundation of his popularity was so broad and so sturdy. The popular press fastened onto his exotic appearance and the trappings of his success. The poet Alfred Nossig, who wrote the libretto of Paderewski's opera *Manru*, was impressed by his bearing:

There is such mastery, such self-confident authority in the manner in which he seats himself at the piano, the way in which he strikes the first chords, that he could say of the instrument what the sculptor Puget said of his marble: 'It trembles before me.'[2]

Fifteen-year-old Artur Rubinstein, a guest at Paderewski's Swiss villa at the turn of the century, listened to him practise and was amazed by his diligence:

He was working on the Handel Variations of Brahms, repeating certain difficult passages slowly a hundred times. I noticed that his playing was greatly handicapped by some technical defects, especially in the articulation of his fingers, which resulted in an unbalanced sense of rhythm. After a short lunch, he used to continue practising until seven o'clock. . . . On the last evening, he sat down at one of the pianos in the salon and played for me for about two hours, showing me all sorts of pianistic difficulties, pointing out brilliant fingerings, tricky pedalling and other interesting sidelights. . . .[3]

Violinist Carl Flesch, a rigorous observer, was won over by Paderewski's power of communication:

Here . . . was proof of the supremacy of spirit over matter, of feeling over a partial lack of technique which would have been grave enough in another to stamp the total result as inferior. A subtle spell emanated from

Paderewski's playing which made one gladly forget his technical insuf-
ficiencies and surrender to the hypnotic influence of this powerful
personality.[4]

And Bernard Shaw, writing without whole-hearted approval of
Paderewski's first London appearances in 1890, appreciated

his pleasant spirit and his dash of humour: he carries his genius and his
mission almost jauntily. . . . . His Parisian vogue is not to be wondered
at: he makes a recital as little oppressive as it is the nature of such a thing
to be.[5]

Paderewski's life was unusually full and varied, even by the
measuring stick of the lives examined in the preceding chapters.
There was personal tragedy and fulfilment; political ambition,
success and disillusionment; poverty and wealth; travel further
afield than any of his illustrious predecessors had undertaken;
friendship with royalty, statesmen, artists and men of letters;
agricultural experiments; charitable initiatives; speculative
follies; and above all, decades of unremitting work at the
keyboard.

The Poland in which Ignazy (westernized: Ignace) Jan
Paderewski was born (6 November 1860, Kuryłówka, province of
Podolia) was a land trisected and dominated by the major con-
tinental powers: Russia (which held the part in which Podolia
lay), Prussia and Austro-Hungary. In the Paderewski family the
liberation and reunification of Poland were questions of overwhelming importance. Ignazy's mother died a few months after
his birth; but the boy learned very early that his maternal grandfather, a university professor, had died in a Siberian prison
camp for his anti-Russian beliefs. Jan Paderewski, Ignazy's
father, an estate administrator, spent a year in a Russian prison
for the same reason. Clearly Paderewski's unfailing national-
ism was firmly established in him at a very early age. The
absence of a mother, scarce contact with children his own age (he
was brought up in a remote village inhabited mainly by Jews,
with whom the Paderewskis and the few other local Christians
did not mix socially) and quick intelligence all contributed to the
shaping of a self-sufficient, resolute character.

Ignazy showed signs of musical talent at an early date; but in
his memoirs he dismisses his early music teachers as well-
meaning bunglers and adds that even his instructors at the
Warsaw Conservatory, which he attended from 1872 to 1878,

91

were of little help to his development as a pianist. There he was given the fundamentals of musical theory and was encouraged at various times to compose and to play the flute, oboe, clarinet, bassoon, horn and trombone – anything but the piano! However, his determination seems to have been increased by others' doubts; and at the age of fifteen he even undertook a tour of provincial Polish and Russian towns together with a fellow-student, a violinist. The duo, setting out with no pre-arranged engagements, met with many absurd misadventures and their undertaking failed miserably.

It is possible, however, that Paderewski exaggerated in later years the discouragement heaped upon him by his teachers; for he graduated at the age of eighteen, was allowed to play the Grieg Concerto with the Conservatory orchestra and was soon invited to join the piano faculty. Before turning twenty he had married Antonina Korsakówna, one of his students; but within a year she had died in childbirth, leaving her young husband with a palsied son. 'Even at twenty', said Paderewski many years later, 'one can plumb the heights and depths and feel the pain and mystery of life.'[6]

For the next two years he lived in Berlin, studying composition and making the acquaintance of musicians like Joachim and Rubinstein. Several of his compositions were published by Hugo Bock. It appears to have been in 1884 that the desire to make a career as a pianist took hold of him most forcefully; and with the encouragement of Modjeska he went to Vienna to study with Leschetizky. Although the celebrated pedagogue believed that Paderewski was too old to develop into a successful pianist, he was kind and helpful to his young compatriot. He told him that he had a natural technique, good tone and pedalling, but that his fingers were completely untrained and that he did not know how to work properly. He made him practise elementary finger exercises and Czerny studies under supervision, letting him proceed gradually to more demanding repertoire. During a period of three or four years, part of which time Paderewski spent as a professor at the Strasbourg Conservatory, he had about thirty lessons with Leschetizky, and claimed that in the first few lessons alone he learned more than in all his previous training. He was quite clear and correct in stating that his playing could not be considered representative of the Leschetizky school; but he was just as forthcoming with praise and gratitude for what the older man had done for him. By 1887

Leschetizky began to believe that Paderewski might possibly make some sort of career for himself.

While it was Paderewski's capacity for work which had made Leschetizky's change of opinion possible, Leschetizky had undoubtedly pinpointed the deficiencies in Paderewski's technique and had provided him with the means for overcoming the most pressing problems. It is an axiom of instrumental instruction that there are no shortcuts or magic formulae leading to mastery; but a clear-sighted and canny teacher can sometimes help a gifted student to cut through a whole web of encumbering mechanical and psychological difficulties. Paderewski, in his mid-twenties, could hardly hope to teach his central nervous system to do many of the things it should have been taught fifteen or twenty years earlier; but he could, by constant practice, compensate to some extent for previous inadequacies and find the path to himself, to what was strongest and most individual in himself and in his approach to music. He must have had tremendous stamina, because the amount of time and physical effort he had to devote to sheer, grinding practice, especially at the outset of his career, was far greater than that which most artists, however conscientious they may be, are accustomed to putting into their work. He often worked more than twelve hours a day at the keyboard. 'Towering ambition and youth', he said, made this dedication possible.[7]

Although Paderewski had of course performed publicly on occasion, his début as a mature artist took place at Paris's Salle Erard on 3 May 1888, in a solo recital that included Beethoven's Thirty-two Variations in C minor and Liszt's Sixth Hungarian Rhapsody, among other works. Tchaikovsky, Annette Essipova, the conductors Edouard Colonne and Charles Lamoureux, various crowned heads and other notables were in the audience. I assume that the presence of so many celebrated musicians at a début recital can be explained by the personal interest of Leschetizky and Essipova in the event, while the attendance of the aristocratic element must have owed a great deal to Modjeska's enthusiasm. (Reading between the lines of her memoirs and journals, it is possible to detect a trace of something other than artistic interest on the part of the actress for her young compatriot.) In any case, Paderewski's triumph was so great that he immediately received invitations for other engagements. Fifty years later he noted in his memoirs:

It was a landslide of applause, a landslide of success if you like – and a

93

catastrophe, the responsibility! . . . It was not only unexpected but totally undeserved. I have never been modest, no, because modesty is undervaluation. But I was humble, and I am still humble. My art – that was the important thing – not my personality. But when I realized the effect of that personality, I knew instantly what was in store for me. . . . 'Now I am entering into an inferno', I said to myself. 'This is not heaven, it is hell.' . . . And of course then began the years and years of labour, beyond my strength even, and of suffering. . . . There followed immediately, in the wake of my debut, a great public demand for a second concert. And I had nothing! I had no other programme.[8]

He had taken eight months to study his first programme; the second one was prepared in three weeks; and although it was 'not perfect academically' (according to Paderewski himself), it was another victory for him. He also played the Saint-Saëns Fourth Piano Concerto in an orchestral concert. Soon he was back in Vienna for further coaching from Leschetizky and for a début recital – another outstanding success – at the Bösendorfer Hall. Paris became his home for a while; he returned there for more concerts and made it the base from which he toured elsewhere in France and in Belgium and Holland.

His first recitals and concerts with orchestra in England took place at St James's Hall, London, in May 1890, and were reasonably well received. J. A. Fuller-Maitland wrote years later that Paderewski seemed 'to unite in himself all the greatest qualities of all the great pianists that ever lived. . . . Even then, nearly forty years ago, there was in him a complete insight into music of many different schools. In particular, one performance of the Schumann concerto stands out as reaching very near perfection, although the readings were occasionally different from those of the orthodox Schumann disciples. . . . Of his Chopin there is no need to speak, for it was always ideally beautiful. . . .'[9]

Shaw, despite the kind comments cited earlier, had serious reservations:

He plays as clearly as Von Bülow – or as nearly so as is desirable, and he is much more accurate. He has not enough consideration for the frailty of his instrument; his *fortissimo*, instead of being serious and formidable. . . , is rather violent and elate. He goes to the point at which a piano huddles itself up and lets itself be beaten instead of unfolding the richness and colour of its tone. . . . He began with Mendelssohn, and knocked him about rather unceremoniously; then he took the Harmonious Blacksmith and spoiled it by making it a stalking-horse for his sleight-of-hand – playing it too fast, in fact; then he went on to Schumann's Fantasia, which seems so hard to fathom because there is next to nothing in it; and then the way was cleared for Chopin. His playing of that great composer's studies – three of them – was by far the best thing he did. The other Chopin pieces were not specially well played; and his execution of the Liszt rhapsody at the end was by no means equal to Sophie Menter's. . . .[10]

London eventually became one of Paderewski's favourite cities: he always returned to it with great pleasure, his popularity there increased and he made many friends, particularly among the nobility and with such well-known artists as Sir Lawrence Alma-Tadema and Edward Burne-Jones. In Berlin, which, like London, he visited for the first time as a professional artist in 1890, he was received much more coldly; and in later life he rarely had anything kind to say about Prussia or Prussians. (His contempt for Prussians was equalled only by his inability to tolerate Russians. In his memoirs he tells the story of a dinner with the famed Russian conductor Vasily Safonov, during which the latter drank eight glasses of cognac, two bottles of white wine, a bottle of claret, two bottles of champagne and six large glasses of beer; and he comments that all Safonov's countrymen drank in this way. That is his kindest remark about the Russians.)

When Rubinstein had made his harrowing American tour in 1872, he had undertaken a pioneer's task. Paderewski, arriving in New York in the autumn of 1891, was one of many artists who regularly crossed the Atlantic, taking European music to America and American gold back to Europe. His tour was sponsored by the Steinway Company; but although his repertoire was by now quite extensive, he had not been told in advance exactly what would be expected of him. On landing, he learned that he would have to play six different piano concerti in three concerts within the space of a week! His début took place at Carnegie Hall (which had opened its doors for the first time just six months earlier) with the New York Symphony under the direction of Walter Damrosch; Paderewski's part of the lengthy programme comprised Saint-Saëns's Second Piano Concerto, a group of solo pieces by Chopin (Nocturne in C minor, Prelude in A-flat major, Waltz in C-sharp minor, Etude in C major – Op. 10 No. 7 – Ballade in F major and Polonaise in A-flat major) and Paderewski's own Piano Concerto. As encores he played Liszt's *La Campanella* and Rubinstein's 'Staccato' Etude. Immediately after the concert he went to the Steinway warehouse and spent five hours practising the next day's programme, thanks to the kindness of the night watchman. There was a rehearsal with orchestra in the morning.

After the rehearsal, I practised again all day for the concert. . . . I cannot tell you how I endured it, but the second concert, in spite of my fatigue, was much better than my first one. There was a larger attendance . . . and some real demonstration of public favour. . . . It was a little ray of hope, without which I do not know whether I would have been able to go again that night . . . and prepare for the third rehearsal. I had to play the Rubinstein Concerto and the Chopin E minor Concerto, and some important solo numbers. It was an afternoon concert and it had taken me seventeen hours of the one day to practise. My arms were dropping off. But I could not have rest. I could not cancel or postpone the concert – it was impossible. So I played that Rubinstein Concerto, and the reception was really remarkable, tremendous. That was the real beginning of my career in America.[11]

Paderewski gave several recitals in New York in addition to his orchestral concerts; and he then set out on the first of what would be a great many tours that were to take him all over the North American continent. The first tour ended at the Metropolitan Opera House in New York on 27 March 1892; he played the Schumann Concerto and his own, along with Liszt's Hungarian Fantasia, with the Boston Symphony under Artur Nikisch. He returned to Europe having made a large sum of money and with his success assured.

The following season he made a second tour of America, where his public greeted him with such frenzied admiration that even Modjeska commented ironically about it in a letter to a friend:

Paderewski continues to win ovations and to take in dollars. Such success no virtuoso before him has ever had, not even Rubinstein, which, however, does not mean that Paderewski is greater than Rubinstein. The difference is in the individuality of the artists, unfortunately not only artistic but superficial, and although Paderewski does not surpass Rubinstein in genius, he does possess a personality of the kind that draws to itself crowds, for the most part of the feminine gender. American misses and ladies, to put it plainly, go mad over him. . . .[12]

Newspaper editors also went mad, although theirs was a rather more cold-blooded form of ecstasy. The following notice, written by the well-known journalist and poet Eugene Field and published in the *Chicago News* in 1893, is a lovely example of what was being said about the pianist:

It is rumored that the popular Paderewski is not the spring chicken that his business managers would fain have us believe him to be. We learn from a credible source that he was a suitor for Modjeska's heart and hand as far back as 1864, at which time he was a professor of piano in the Conservatory at Cracow. But he was cut out by Count Charles Bozenta Chłapowski. . . . It is furthermore narrated that the constant practice of eating lemons has given Paderewski's hair the peculiar tint and the still more peculiar willowiness which make it so remarkable a feature of the artist. [13]

One wonders what those Kraków students thought of their four-year-old professor – or Chłapowski of his precocious rival.

But a great deal was written about Paderewski in the American press that did not have to do with his hair or with the hysteria he induced in his most enraptured admirers. One of the most interesting articles appeared in *The Century* magazine. It was written by William Mason, who had been a pupil of Liszt and who had heard most of the great pianists of the day. He called Paderewski

a thoroughly earnest and at the same time an affectionate player, and too much stress cannot be laid on the humanism of his style, which is intensely sympathetic, and so eclectic that it embraces all schools. His never failing warmth of touch and his vivid appreciation of tone gradations and values result in wonderfully beautiful effects. . . . His magnetic individuality . . . is felt and acknowledged even by those who do not entirely and uniformly approve of all of his readings. . . . Paderewski has an advantage over Rubinstein . . . in the fact that he is always master of his resources and possesses power of complete self-control. . . . The glissando octave passages near the end of the C Major Sonata, Op. 53 ['Waldstein'], he performs as originally designed by Beethoven, notwithstanding Dr Hans von Bülow's assertion that this method of execution is impossible on our modern pianos. . . . In many passages . . . he ingeniously manages to bring out the full rhythmic and metrical effect, also the emphasis necessary to discriminatory fingering, effected either by interlocking the hands or by dividing different portions of the runs and arpeggios between them. [14]

Alfredo Colombani, who heard Paderewski play in Milan in 1897, also felt that the pianist's technique was superb; but in a

97

review in the *Corriere della Sera* (2–3 February) he complained that what that technique achieved often seemed to be at odds, and arbitrarily so, with the character of the music it was supposed to be serving. He insisted that

> . . . classical music does not lend itself to bizarre interpretations, even if these are intended as a means of bringing merited recognition to an exceptional performer. . . . By request, Paderewski had to repeat a Chopin Study. It was easily noticed that he played the piece much more quickly the second time through. Perhaps I am pedantic, but I cannot adjust myself to this notion of *ever more difficult.* . . .

Others, too, had reservations; and Richard Aldrich expressed some of them in *The New York Times* in 1905:

> . . . there is much in Mr. Paderewski's playing that ought not to be there. . . . Some of the pounding that he did yesterday was scandalous and knew no measure; and this was never an element in Paderewski's spell in those earlier days. He can still coax tone of an ineffable beauty from the instrument; but he likewise forces it, continually and repeatedly, to a harsh and wiry jangling that has nothing musical in its quality. It seems as if in some way he lost something of that instinctive sense of proportion that used to characterize everything he did. He makes at times excessive contrasts, seeks exaggerated climaxes, obvious effects. The aristocratic refinement, the delicate reserve of his playing has been encroached upon. . . .[15]

Paderewski's life began to assume the outline that most performers' lives assume: lengthy tours interrupted by periods of repose and study. In addition to his annual visits to North America, he travelled to places where even the courageous Anton Rubinstein would not have considered setting foot – South America, Australia, New Zealand and South Africa. He commanded enormous fees, and even condescended to perform at private soirées in Britain and on the Continent when the price was right and when the hosts pledged their guests' silence. There was, however, a high price to be paid on his part as well for this frenzied activity: at various times in his career he suffered from acute stage fright, severe muscle and tendon strain and a form of depression that manifested itself in hatred of the piano.

Regarding the first problem, Paderewski had a theory:

> Fright, that terrible inside nervousness, practically fear of everything, of the public, of the piano, of the conditions and of the memory too, was nothing else but a bad conscience. For years and years I had it. . . .

98

Fright is only the sense of insecurity, and it may be insecurity of only one passage or phrase. . . . You may play ten pieces on a programme perfectly, without a blunder, they are absolutely under your control, but if the eleventh is not in perfect condition, let us say, and even one little phrase or a few bars of a great composition remain unconquered, and elude the fingers, it is quite enough to upset your whole inner being. . . . When I realized this and came to more mature years, I practised quite differently. I found the right way. Of course, in any public appearance, there is always the usual nervousness, but that is quite a different thing. . . . [16]

The physical problems were related to specific incidents and were cured by rest and therapy; but the psychological disturbance was a more difficult one. Moreover, it lasted intermittently from 1906 to 1912. Again, we have Paderewski's own words:

. . . Something was happening to my nerves that made me completely *hate* the piano. I loathed it. I do not know if there was any one particular cause to which I could attribute that feeling. . . . Still I was obliged to play, and naturally, it showed in my playing. Yes, I felt it deeply. It was so very inferior to my past performances. . . . [I] tried all kinds of treatments, not only doctors and their medicines but every suggestion even. There was a famous physician at Lausanne, who treated me (or tried to treat me) without any result. Another physician here [in Switzerland] hypnotized me in hopes of a cure, but that was no good. . . . The easiest pieces I had in my repertoire I could not manage. My fingers were just like cotton. I could not produce the tone. [17]

Fortunately, the problem disappeared with the passage of time.

Paderewski's tours – particularly his American tours – had made him a wealthy man by the time he reached his mid-thirties. He bought a huge estate in the Austrian-held Polish province of Galicia, but soon had to sell it at a loss. For a while he owned and administered an experimental farm in Switzerland, which was also sold when it became a financial liability. Years later he bought a large ranch at Paso Robles, California, at whose thermal springs and mud baths he had once been cured of muscular pains. His intention was to develop the property; but it, too, cost him a great deal of money. As a patriotic Pole, he invested some of his fortune in Polish industries which lost their value at the beginning of the First World War. He was a generous man and gave away vast sums to charities, artistic funds and individuals. But the expenditure which gave him most lasting pleasure was the purchase of a chalet, Riond-Bosson, near Morges (Lausanne). This was his principal home for over forty years.

In 1899 Paderewski married Helena Gorska (*née* Baroness de Rosen), the former wife of one of his Warsaw schoolmates. Modjeska, in her memoirs, implies that Mme Gorska and Paderewski had been lovers as early as 1884; and Paderewski admits in his own memoirs that it was she who had taken care of his invalid son for many years. He takes great pains to point out that although he was then and always remained completely opposed to divorce, Mme Gorska's divorce, which had made his marriage to her possible, was somehow an exceptional case. He brought his new wife and nineteen-year-old son to Riond-Bosson; but Alfred Paderewski, victim since childhood of a debilitating disease, died two years later.

Paderewski had a marked taste for refined living. It is interesting to observe major artists when they find themselves mixing at various times with what are generally referred to as the upper echelons of society: some of them are repelled by what they see, others indifferent to it, still others greatly entertained by it. Paderewski was different: he wished to emulate the aristocratic way of life, and he succeeded in doing so. His enormous fortune, fine manners and natural self-assurance made this possible; and his home at Riond-Bosson resembled in many respects the country estate of a monarch. Every day, when he was not on tour, the household – family, guests and staff – would assemble at noon in the great hall. Fred Gaisberg, the recording pioneer who was responsible for Paderewski's and many other artists' commitment to the gramophone, said that 'at one o'clock the Master descended the staircase smiling, and greeted each person present with a few apt enquiries about their health and activities. It resembled a small court. He then led the way to the dining-room where, seated at the head of the table, he saw that everyone was cared for.'[18] The piano, in the music room, was surmounted by autographed photographs of kings and queens, from Victoria onwards. There was even a private billiards parlour in the mansion. (Paderewski was a devotee of both billiards and bridge.) 'I shall never forget', wrote Gaisberg, 'the great revels held on Paderewski's Saint's Day, the Feast of St. Ignatius, when, in addition to his neighbours, friends assembled from all over Europe to join in the celebrations. The grounds were hung with festoons and flags. There was great feasting and music, and in the evening we had fireworks. These fetes were carried out in a truly regal way, as befitted his wealth and position.'[19]

There is endless testimony to the fact that Paderewski was a very well-read and highly intelligent man, who was always interested in increasing his knowledge. Even in his last years, he took lessons to improve his Spanish in order to be able to read the works of Unamuno. On the other hand, he does not seem to have been directly involved with the main musical, literary or artistic movements of his day or with their leading figures, despite his friendship, referred to earlier, with artists like Alma-Tadema and Burne-Jones. The people to whom he was most attracted, apart from royalty, were statesmen; and the results of that interest helped to form an important and very unusual chapter in his life.

It was during one of his periods of withdrawal from the piano that Paderewski first became actively engaged in Polish politics. Since childhood he had dreamed of erecting a monument to the Poles who had triumphed over the Germans at the Battle of Grünwald in 1410. In 1908 he commissioned Antoni Wiwulski, a young Polish sculptor, to create such a monument, which was unveiled in Kraków on the five hundredth anniversary of the battle. Paderewski made a speech at the dedication ceremony; and later that year he gave another patriotic address in Lwów on the occasion of the centenary of Chopin's birth.

When the First World War broke out, Paderewski sensed that the time was ripe to press for the establishment of a free and independent Poland. Many Polish refugees visited him at Riond-Bosson; he helped to form a Polish Aid Committee in nearby Vevey; and in London he and Alma-Tadema's daughter organized the Polish Victims' Relief Fund. From there he proceeded to America, where he initiated a fund-raising tour. In addition to concerts and recitals, he gave over three hundred speeches on Poland's behalf during a two-year period. Because of his high connections (he was, for example, personally acquainted with Asquith, Balfour, Lloyd George and other major British political figures) he was able to put his views before President Wilson at private meetings. When Germany and Austria proposed the creation of a Free Poland without the provinces of Silesia, Pomerania and Poznania, Paderewski persuaded Wilson to oppose the offer; and early in 1917 the president declared that Poland must be united and independent, with free access to the Baltic assured – a statement that later became the thirteenth of his famous Fourteen Points. As soon as the United States entered the war Paderewski helped to subsidize the foundation of a Free Polish army, consisting of over twenty thousand Polish Americans.

Immediately after the Armistice he returned to Poland. The country's provisional leader, General Józef Piłsudski, saw that Paderewski was popular with the people and trusted by the victorious powers, who liked his strong anti-Socialism. (Piłsudski himself was somewhat tainted in their eyes by his Socialist connections.) He invited Paderewski to form a non-partisan government in Warsaw; and so from January to November 1919 the world's most famous pianist was prime minister and foreign minister of a reborn Poland. Although Paderewski was loosely associated with nationalistic and conservative groups whose policies were based on free enterprise, strong central government and, to some extent, anti-Semitism, he did not enjoy the backing of any single party.* It appears, too, that he found the ungentlemanly aspects of politics – opposition to his views, for example – distasteful; and so his attempt late in 1921 to be elected president of Poland was unsuccessful and he left his country forever – with the exception of a visit to Poznań in 1924 to receive an honorary doctorate from the university.

After four years away from the keyboard he resumed concert activity in 1922. He was now in his sixties, and reports on his playing vary widely. Fuller-Maitland heard him in the mid-'20s and said:

I felt that never had I heard such depth of expression, such richness of phrasing, or such insight into the whole world of music. That he should have reconquered all the wonderful technique of the past was amazing

---

*Paderewski's position on the political spectrum can be adequately illustrated by two examples. He tells in his memoirs of a trip to Mexico in 1899 during which he met that country's dictator, Porfirio Diaz. Diaz made 'a great impression' on him: 'He was indeed a remarkable man. As long as he was there the country was orderly and prosperous. He was just the man for those people, an iron-handed man. At that time there were no bandits – there was perfect peace and order in the whole country.' And during the 1920s and even into the '30s Paderewski repeatedly called on Mussolini during his Italian tours. 'I think he is a very great statesman', he told his biographer, Rom Landau. 'I am a great admirer both of Mussolini and of Italian Fascism.'[20]

enough, but it was a far greater surprise to find that he was on a higher artistic plane than before. All the intimate and controlled emotion of Clara Schumann, all the power of Rubinstein – though with none of the jars that came from the tortured strings under that giant – and all the intellectual grasp of Bülow, were there in the fullest measure. . . .[21]

But Artur Rubinstein heard Paderewski in Paris just a few years later and came away with quite a different opinion:

Paderewski's concert was typical of his public appearances. He made us wait as usual, and when he finally appeared, executed his famous deep bows a dozen times, and then settled down to a Chopin programme. I cannot remember all of it, but the A-flat Polonaise, with which he finished the recital, had his fists banging the bass notes without discrimination. Then something strange happened. The public was applauding without much enthusiasm, politely awaiting an encore; when Paderewski reappeared, he bowed almost to the floor until the applause grew stronger and stronger, then he settled down and played four encores in succession without letting his public leave the hall. It remained in my memory as a sad concert.[22]

The subject of Paderewski's playing at this period prompted some comments from Artur Schnabel during an interview some years later:

Voice: Did you ever hear Paderewski play professionally?

Mr Schnabel: He played *only* professionally.

Voice: But did you ever hear him?

Mr Schnabel: Yes, I heard him once.

Voice: I have heard people tell how in his concerts a crew of three or four men would come out on the stage before he played to measure the height of the piano stool, its distance from the piano, and so forth.

Mr Schnabel: I have never heard that about Paderewski. I heard that [Vladimir de] Pachmann had a distinct inclination towards clownery in his concerts; but Paderewski was solemnity itself. He and Fritz Kreisler always appeared as if Atlas had had an easy task in comparison – as if they bore all the sorrows of mankind. At the time I heard Paderewski, in Los Angeles, he had apparently passed the peak of his pianistic career. It was after he had interrupted playing for years. I enjoyed the second half of the concert [i.e., the 'lighter' pieces] very much, the first half not so much.[23]

Fortunately, one need not base one's ideas of Paderewski's playing entirely on hearsay, for he was one of the first major instrumentalists to record extensively. Between 1911, when he was fifty, and 1938, when he was seventy-seven, he made about one hundred recordings, not including piano rolls; and they present a remarkably interesting and varied picture of his work.

It is immediately clear that the stories of Paderewski's technical inadequacies are true. No pianist with his keyboard problems could hope to have a successful career today. This is not to denigrate either Paderewski or our contemporaries: it is a simple statement of fact. Complete technical security obviously does not ensure fine musicianship; nevertheless, even the most extraordinary musical qualities can be obscured or destroyed through faulty presentation.

The recordings demonstrate that Paderewski's greatest technical accomplishments were his quick and delicate right-hand passage-work – scales, glissandi and so on. Where his technique often let him down was in heavier, complicated chord passages, octave passages and the like. Distinguishing marks of Paderewski's playing were his frequent separation of left and right hands – something which modern listeners are unaccustomed to, but which was common enough in Paderewski's youth and earlier – and a freedom of movement within the basic tempo he chose for a given piece or section of a piece.

His first recording, the Chopin A major Polonaise, dates from 1911 and is unimpressive. It contains frequent, grating mistakes in the bigger chords and does not compensate with a particularly interesting overall performance. One would be inclined to attribute the poor playing to the piano-phobia which he was going through at the time, if it did not perfectly match Artur Rubinstein's description of Paderewski's playing of another polonaise twenty years later.

In 1912 Paderewski made a number of recordings; and they tell a less one-sided story. Some of Chopin's Etudes, Op. 25, are very beautiful – No. 1 in A-flat major, No. 2 in F minor and particularly No. 7 in C-sharp minor, which is played with great delicacy. There is a noble sadness to the tone, no wallowing sentimentality. His use of *rubato* is not excessive: even at dramatic moments, the tempo is reasonably steady. Those of the Op. 10 Etudes which I have heard are less successful: No. 3 in E major is lovely in tone but rhythmically very distorted, and the climaxes are wild and brutal; No. 7 in C major is very graceful but also very slow; and No. 12 in C minor ('Revolutionary') contains much inaccurate and unsteady playing. The Mazurka in A minor, Op. 19 No. 3, however, is stunning, played with warmth and lightness.

Three excerpts from Schumann's *Fantasiestücke*, Op. 12, were also recorded in 1912 and are extremely interesting. Paderewski plays *Des Abends* in a slow, dreamy tempo and with a gentle, clear tone. His 'orchestral' treatment of the inner voices is especially beautiful. The beginning of *Aufschwung* is played with a distorting *rubato*, but the lyrical parts are lovely. He pulls the middle section somewhat out of shape, despite which the performance maintains its own internal logic. One often hears wrong notes in the more difficult passages. In *Warum?* Paderewski demonstrates a wonderful feeling for sound and for the contours of the piece's harmonic movement. The rhetoric is sometimes exaggerated; but there is a pervading feeling of great intimacy in the presentation.

A 1917 recording of Chopin's Nocturne in F-sharp major, Op. 15 No. 2, shows Paderewski slowing down at the end of the first period and taking his time over all the embellishing figures. The short chromatic-scale ornaments (bars 18 and 20) are hair-raisingly beautiful. He plays the middle section with great restraint and uses the pedal sparingly; and the ending is superb. The Waltz in A-flat major, Op. 42, recorded in 1922 is played with great poise; but a recording, made the same year, of Liszt's Hungarian Rhapsody No. 10, despite some amazing glissandi, is awful in the technically demanding parts.

Schubert's B-flat major Impromptu, Op. 142 No. 3, recorded in 1924, repeats a now familiar story: the lighter and more delicate sections are played with exceptional grace, but the more dramatic sections seem almost to fall apart at times. In the first movement of Beethoven's 'Moonlight' Sonata (1926), Paderewski's custom of sometimes playing the left hand before the right is very much in evidence. He maintains a forward momentum and even presses the tempo a bit in the passage leading to the climax; and he often prepares his cadences by making slight *ritenuti*. As in *Des Abends*, the balance among the voices is exquisite. There is also a recording dating from 1930 of four of Debussy's Préludes, Book I: *Danseuses de Delphes, Voiles, Le Vent dans la plaine* and *Minstrels*. The first three are beautifully conceived but somewhat heavy-handed; *Minstrels* is played with great humour but, again, the chord passages are ponderous.

The overall impression which these recordings make is that of a highly intelligent artist with definite and extremely individual-istic musical ideas. What is true of attitudes towards other great performing musicians is also true in regard to Paderewski: when one agrees with his musical conception, one is delighted and moved by the performance; when one does not, one must still respect the integrity behind that conception.

During the 1920s and '30s Paderewski divided most of his time between his American tours (winter and spring) and Riond-Bosson (summer and autumn). It was his custom to spend a few weeks in the spring relaxing at his California ranch. He visited Australia for a second time in 1927 and made a major European tour in 1929. Later that year he underwent an emergency appendectomy, and his recovery was retarded by a severe attack of phlebitis. A whole year passed before he could resume touring.

His powers as a pianist were declining, and the death of his wife early in 1934 was a blow to his spirits. The German invasion of Poland in 1939 upset him greatly; he had a radio installed at Riond-Bosson so that he could follow the events of the war more closely. Finally, in the autumn of 1940, he could remain still no longer, and departed for the United States to raise money for Polish relief. There he passed his eightieth birthday in November. His health was delicate and he spent the winter in Palm Beach, Florida. The Polish parliament-in-exile made him its president, and he spoke in public and on the radio pleading for money for the Poles. Early in 1941 President Roosevelt proclaimed a 'Paderewski Week' in honour of the fiftieth anniversary of the pianist's first American tour. Paderewski returned to New York in May, but contracted pneumonia a month later and died on 29 June 1941 in his suite at the Buckingham Hotel. At Roosevelt's order, he was buried in Arlington National Cemetery with full military honours.

Paderewski remains one of the strangest phenomena in the history of the piano. He was never influenced strongly enough by any teacher to be classifiable as 'pupil of' so-and-so; and his interpretative manner was so personal, his technique so spotty, that we cannot label any of his successors – even those who admired him greatly – as examples of the 'school of' Paderewski. He stood and indeed wished to stand alone; and in his prime his name was associated with the piano in much the same way as Liszt's had been two generations earlier. A great many serious musicians were completely won over by him. British pianist Harriet Cohen wrote that his 'wide, deeply set green eyes, often half-closed, were mesmeric; the features noble. The bearing was majestic, yet modest. This was a King among men.'[24] And another pianist, the well-known accompanist André Benoist, described a small dinner party in London at which Paderewski spontaneously offered to play.

. . . The grand 'gentleman of music' walked to the piano and for one hour entertained us with music by Chopin. . . . It was such playing as one dreams of but seldom hears. Absent was all showmanship. Absent was all self-consciousness. There remained only the great artist completely immersed in the music. . . .[25]

One is tempted to comment cynically about art concealing art, about the apparent absence of showmanship being, in fact, the most subtle form of showmanship. But such a remark would be unjust, even if there were some truth in it. One cannot be a performer unless one performs. There are musicians who give the impression of boredom when they play, others who look like contenders for Olympic gold medals, or prestidigitators – or worse. If some of Paderewski's effectiveness was achieved through an attitude of dignified concentration, one would be churlish to complain. And the intensely poetic qualities which can still be heard in many of his recordings offer an even better explanation of the impact he made on the musical world of his time.

Chapter 5

Fritz Kreisler

❖❖❖❖❖❖❖❖❖❖❖❖❖❖❖❖❖❖❖❖❖❖❖❖❖❖❖❖❖❖❖❖❖❖❖❖❖

They wrote me from home that the wife of our family physician, Dr Kreisler, is in Paris; I should have called on her long ago. I have just been there, rue Bleue in the Faubourg Poissonière next to the Conservatoire. The unfortunate woman has a ten-year-old son who, after two years in the Vienna Conservatorium, won the great prize there and is said to be highly gifted. Now instead of secretly throttling the prodigy the wretched father, who is over-worked and has a house full of children, has sent the boy with his mother to Paris to study at the Conservatoire and try for another prize. Just imagine the expense, the separation, the dispersal of the household! Needless to say the poor woman, who is giving up everything for the boy, is bored to tears. Little wonder that parents grow vain about their children, and even less that such children grow vain themselves. . . . The prodigy is pale, plain, but looks pretty intelligent.

Letter of Sigmund Freud (26 November 1885)
to his fiancée, Martha Bernays

IN THE END, Dr Samuel Severin Kreisler turned out to have been right, and his friend Dr Freud need not have worried. Dr Kreisler's son Friedrich, better known as Fritz, was to demonstrate that the efforts made on his behalf were not in vain.

The most malicious of biographers or historians would be hard put to find an unkind comment about Fritz Kreisler, the man or the artist. His colleagues not only respected and admired him, they loved him as well. A generous, unassuming person, he played the violin with warmth, vitality and formidable technique. He was an all-round musician – a competent pianist, composer and arranger – who also had a wide-ranging knowledge of other spheres of human activity.

Kreisler follows Paderewski in this book by chronological coincidence. In other respects the juxtaposition is odd and even amusing, for it would be hard to conceive of two more dissimilar artists. Where Paderewski struggled all his adult life to achieve and maintain a high level of technical proficiency,

Kreisler did his spade work as a small child and spent the rest of his life avoiding the violin except when he was actually performing or playing for his own pleasure. ('Practising', he said, 'is nothing but a bad habit.') Paderewski was the noble-souled artist, lofty, somewhat remote, who revealed his musical visions to an awe-struck public, while Kreisler seemed to take his listeners by the arm and communicate with them in an intimate, friendly way. And where Paderewski's private life seems to have been essentially sober and inextricably bound up with patriotic causes, the Kreisler tale is one of extremes: a wild, dissipated youth, followed by a long, steady marriage which was kept entirely away from the limelight.

Fritz learned to read music when he was three (he was born in Vienna on 2 February 1875) and soon made himself an imitation violin out of a cigarbox and shoelaces, in order to pretend to play correctly what he had heard his father's amateur string quartet playing incorrectly. Kreisler Senior was a frustrated musician who had turned to medicine only at his father's insistence. 'That I became a musician', said the violinist in later years, 'may be due to the fact that he projected, perhaps unconsciously, his own unfulfilled wish on to me.'[2] Fritz was taught violin first by his father and then by Jacques Auber, leader of the Ring Theatre orchestra. He became a student at the Vienna Conservatory in 1882 – the first time anyone under the age of ten had been admitted. That same year he performed in public for the first time, sharing a concert at Carlsbad Spa with the singer Carlotta Patti, sister of Adelina. At the Conservatory he studied violin with Joseph Hellmesberger the Younger and theory with Anton Bruckner; he taught himself the piano and became so proficient that Paderewski commented, many years later, 'I would be starving if Kreisler had taken up the piano.'[3]

A wealth of musical experiences was available to Kreisler and his Viennese contemporaries. As a boy he was able to hear Joachim, Sarasate, Rubinstein and many others; and his father's circle of friends – apart from Freud, with whom Dr Kreisler played chess – included the composer Károly Goldmark and Dr Theodor Billroth, the well-known surgeon who was also a highly competent musician and a close friend of Brahms.

As Freud informed us, it was at the age of ten that Fritz won the gold medal (first prize) for violin at the Conservatory. The other entrants were much older than he. He was given a three-quarters-size Amati by friends and went off to Paris to study at

109

that city's Conservatory. Joseph Massart, former pupil of Beethoven's friend Rodolphe Kreutzer, accepted him as a student; and Massart soon wrote to Fritz's father that although he had been 'the teacher of Wieniawski and many others . . . little Fritz will be the greatest of them all.'[4] The boy's composition teacher was Léo Delibes who, however, was more interested in skirt-chasing than in teaching. Kreisler later reported that Delibes would 'hand me the beginning of some composition on which he happened to be at work, suggest that I try to catch the spirit of it, and then charge me with going on from there. . . .'[5] (He maintained that it was he rather than Delibes himself who had composed the motif of the celebrated waltz from *Coppélia*; but here Kreisler's outstanding ability as a *raconteur* seems to have run a bit wild, since *Coppélia* was composed five years before Fritz's birth.) César Franck was among the musicians whom the boy met in Paris; and he played in the Pasdeloup Orchestra during his stay in the city. In 1887, at the age of twelve, Fritz won first prize for violin at the Conservatory, despite the fact that he was a decade younger than most of the other prize-winners; and there ended his formal musical training.

The following year, accompanied by his mother, he toured America with the Polish pianist and former Liszt pupil Moriz Rosenthal. His début took place in Boston on 9 November 1888, when he played the Mendelssohn Concerto and Ernst's 'Hungarian Airs'. The conductor was Walter Damrosch. In New York the following night he again played the Mendelssohn Concerto, this time with Anton Seidl conducting. Concerts as far west as Kansas City and as far south as New Orleans followed. On his return to Vienna he spent two years at a classical Gymnasium and also received tutoring in Greek, Latin and physics from his father. He then decided to study medicine, and at one period he thought seriously of pursuing a military career. Although he maintained a lifelong curiosity about all these areas and others as well (philosophy in particular), he eventually decided to concentrate on music. Arnold Rosé, who was leader of the Vienna Hofoper Orchestra (Vienna Philharmonic for concerts) from 1881 to 1938, heard Kreisler audition for a position in that ensemble and turned him down. The reason for this rejection is not known.

After a tour of Russia, during which he met César Cui, Alexander Glazunov and other leading musicians, Kreisler was fortunate enough to arouse the interest of a manufacturer named

Posselt, who became his benefactor and began to sponsor his appearances. Following a performance of the Bruch Concerto with the Vienna Philharmonic under Hans Richter in December 1898 he received the warm compliments of old Hanslick, who wrote in the *Neue Freie Presse* that the young violinist was a 'finished master' capable of 'brilliant virtuosity'. Three months later Kreisler made a successful Berlin début and returned there in December 1899 to play the Mendelssohn Concerto with Nikisch and the Berlin Philharmonic.

It is surprising that a musician who had made such an outstanding beginning as a child should have had to wait until he was about twenty-five for true international recognition. Part of the explanation lies in the diversified intellectual interests which occupied his attention during his younger years, and which he later considered to have been of the greatest importance to his artistic development; but he also led quite an undisciplined personal life during the 1890s, which held back the progress of his career. He participated in the 'artistic' café life of his native city and was able to get to know such figures as Brahms, Kalbeck, Hanslick, Hofmannsthal, Liliencron, Schnitzler, Hugo Wolf, Schoenberg and Wedekind; but he also plunged wholeheartedly into the vices Vienna offered – gambling, drinking, high living. He was involved in numerous affairs with women, too, and this way of life continued until he was married in 1902. His wife, Harriet Lies Woerz, an American divorcée of German descent, brought discipline to his life. She was beautiful, witty, tough and extremely outspoken. Under her influence Kreisler began to concentrate on his career and learned to take care of himself, to marshal his strength. She could be jealous and difficult; but Kreisler, who was essentially a gentle and disorganized man, came to depend on her entirely. 'I am afraid of people and life as a whole', he admitted;[6] and of his wife's part in his career he said simply: 'She made me.'

Even before his marriage Kreisler had achieved success in America – where, in December 1900, he had played for the first time since his appearances as a child of thirteen – and in Britain (début, May 1902). he began touring Europe on a regular basis and became friendly with such artists as Antonio Scotti, Harold Bauer, Jacques Thibaud, Wilhelm Backhaus and Ernö Dohnányi. When Kreisler returned to America in January 1905 Richard Aldrich wrote in *The New York Times*:

. . . he has attained a position incontestably among the great ones in his art. He has grown in every way – in technical power, in depth of feeling and poetic insight, in repose, in largeness of view, in breadth of sympathy that put him upon the level of the highest mastery. . . . If there ever was any of the dross of virtuosoship in Mr Kreisler's artistic nature, he has purified himself of it; and he showed himself last evening as a true interpreter in the highest sense, standing always sincerely for the music he was engaged with and concerned not at all with that which makes for display. . . . His left hand is of remarkable fluency and accuracy; and inaccuracies of intonation . . . were most rare. His bowing is free and firm and moulded to express the subtlest nuances of phrase and of dynamics. . . . [7]

During a tour of Russia in 1914 Kreisler was overwhelmed by the playing of thirteen-year-old Jascha Heifetz, whom he heard in Leopold Auer's class at the St Petersburg Conservatory. Shortly afterwards he told the American violinist Albert Spalding that he was thinking of giving up playing;[8] and to Efrem Zimbalist (another former Auer pupil) he is reported to have said: 'You and I might as well break our violins over our knees now.' But despite Heifetz's great international success, Kreisler's own career was never obfuscated by that of his younger colleague. Moreover, Heifetz, a difficult man, is said to have maintained a life-long love of and admiration for Kreisler – sentiments which he seems not to have felt for many of his fellow violinists.

At the outbreak of the First World War the Austrian army immediately ordered Kreisler to report for duty. He was mistakenly reported killed in action at the battle of Lemberg (Lwów) on 14 September 1914; but in fact he had only sustained a serious leg wound. After a period in hospital he returned to the United States – still a neutral power at that time – and began to play again. With his wife's encouragement, he undertook to support forty-three war orphans and to give financial assistance to fifteen hundred European artists and students, as well as participating in a great number of charity concerts. Once the United States had entered the war, the protests over Kreisler's continued appearances (he was officially an enemy alien) became too strong to be ignored, and he cancelled all engagements excepting charitable events. During the unanticipated free time now available to him he wrote an operetta (*Apple Blossoms*, first performed in 1919).

112

12. Ignace Jan Paderewski (1860–1941) may have been a late developer but when he finally began to make his way, in his late twenties, his success was extraordinary. His powerful personality and romantic appearance, combined with the poetic quality of his playing – when he was at his best – brought him fame and fortune. Here he is shown in an American caricature of the 1890s.

13, 14. (*Opposite*) Paderewski at about the age of forty – the successful
virtuoso with aristocratic tastes. (*Above*) A constant element in his life
was his intense devotion to his country, Poland. During the First World
War he cultivated his political acquaintances and persuaded President
Wilson to support the idea of a free and united Polish nation. From
January to November 1919, the world's most famous pianist was prime
minister and foreign minister of a reborn Poland. Here he and his wife
are seen leaving the Château de Saint-Germain during the peace
conference of 1919.

15. Following his failure to be elected President of Poland, Paderewski resumed his concert activities. Although his powers were declining, he continued to play all over the world. He also made many recordings, and at the age of seventy-five he starred in a film entitled *Moonlight Sonata*. (*Below*) Paderewski with director Lothar Mendes on the set of the film (January 1936).

16. When Germany occupied Poland at the beginning of the Second
World War, Paderewski became head of the Polish National Committee.
He went to the United States in 1940 to raise money for Polish relief. In
the photo Paderewski is making an address on the NBC radio network
from his suite in the Buckingham Hotel, 16 May 1941. This is one of the
last photographs of him: he died at the end of June.

17, 18. Two portrait photographs of Fritz Kreisler (1875–1962), one of the greatest and most influential violinists of the century and one of the musicians most beloved of his colleagues and the public. Kreisler had graduated from the Vienna Conservatory at the age of ten and from the Paris Conservatory at twelve, and had then turned his attention to other areas before making up his mind to follow a musical career. We see him (*opposite*) in the early days of his success, when the warmth and intensity of his tone were beginning to change people's ideas about violin technique. (*Above*) Kreisler at the height of his career.

19. Although Kreisler lived to be nearly eighty-seven, his playing began to deteriorate when he was in his sixties. This photograph shows him at a party given in honour of his seventy-fifth birthday in 1950, which was also the year of his last public performances.

Kreisler waited nearly a year after the termination of hostilities before reappearing in New York. Aldrich described his first postwar concert in this *New York Times* article (27 October 1919):

Mr Fritz Kreisler . . . returned to the concert platform yesterday afternoon and found a welcome of overwhelming enthusiasm awaiting him. Carnegie Hall was filled to its utmost capacity – to more than its capacity – and several hundred would-be listeners were turned away. . . . He returns, so far as was disclosed by yesterday's concert, with his art in all of its manifestations unimpaired, in technical skill, in the plastic eloquence of his bowing, in the accuracy of his intonation, in the excellence of his tone. Above and beyond all this, which may be taken for granted, is the spiritual insight, the musical feeling that touches everything he does – all his well remembered qualities that have impressed his art so deeply upon the public. About them there is nothing new to say. [9]

His reappearance in London on 4 May 1921 was greeted with similar enthusiasm by Ernest Newman in the *Sunday Times*:

The scene in Queen's Hall was the most extraordinary I have ever witnessed. . . . In the whole of my concert-going career I can recall no such welcome to any artist. . . . Kreisler comported himself through it all with the simple dignity one might have expected of him. . . . Kreisler is greater than ever. There is not a violinist in the world who can approach him. [10]

In 1923 Kreisler toured the Far East, playing with success in many Chinese, Japanese, Korean and Manchurian cities. That same year, at the height of Germany's dreadful inflation crisis, Kreisler and his wife paid for one hot meal a day for between six and eight hundred children in Berlin; and in 1924 they moved into a new home in that city. Other unusual events of the 1920s included a tour of Hawaii, Australia and New Zealand in the spring of 1925 and a huge benefit concert at the Metropolitan Opera House in March 1927 to aid cancer research. (The sum of $26,000 was realized.) Kreisler turned down an invitation to give concerts in the USSR in 1931 because he disagreed with the Soviet system; but he did not hesitate to dine with Mussolini during one of his frequent Italian tours in that same period. There was a South American tour in the spring of 1925 – with both transatlantic crossings made aboard the *Graf Zeppelin*.

The Kreislers were so in love with their Berlin home that they fled Germany only when war appeared imminent; however, he had refused to play in Nazi Germany from the outset. And despite his strong patriotic feelings towards Austria, he became a French citizen after the *Anschluss* in 1938.

During the Second World War he and his wife made their home in New York; and one day in 1941 the sixty-six-year-old violinist was hit by a delivery van while crossing Madison Avenue at 57th Street. He suffered a brain concussion and was in a coma for four weeks. After a year-long convalescence he resumed concert activity. (The one lasting effect of his accident was an inability to remember the events of his life from 1928 to 1930 and from 1933 to 1936.) Because he refused to accept a passport from the French Vichy government, he again changed nationalities and became an American citizen in 1943. In later years his playing began to deteriorate and his last public appearances were radio broadcasts during the 1949–50 season. He died in New York on 29 January 1962 at the age of nearly eighty-seven.

As early as 1910 Kreisler had explained his success – in answer to a question from the American music critic H. T. Finck – as follows:

. . . in reviewing the influences that made me, I really can only see three great outstanding powerful factors: (1) my work, (2) my wife's love and help, and (3) my robust health. (1) My work branches into musical and general studies (such as philosophy, history, natural sciences, mathematics, Greek, Latin, and modern languages), and I am inclined to lay more stress on the ultimate beneficial influence of my general studies. My work in the sphere of music subdivides itself into purely violinistic and general musical studies (such as musical science, instrumentation, knowledge of the great symphonic and operatic masterworks, chamber music, piano playing, score reading, etc.), and here again I attach more importance to my *general* musical training than to the purely violinistic, as probably the more powerful factor in making me.

(2) and (3). As to the other two great influences in my life, the love and help of my dear wife and companion, and my robust health, I can only humbly and thankfully acknowledge their tremendous power in the making of me, without any further comment, which might, I fear, discourage such colleagues and students as have not been blessed with the gift of those two invaluable treasures. [11]

But of course it was Kreisler's unique style of playing which 'made him', which secured for him a special place in the history of the violin. Carl Flesch, that wonderfully astute observer, heard Kreisler play Thomé's *Adagio religioso* at an audition in 1895. (Flesch was twenty-two, Kreisler twenty at the time.)

. . . for the first time I gained some notion of Kreisler's greatness and originality: his performance of this piece of saccharine was one of the strongest impressions of my life. Of religious feeling, to be sure, there was no trace: rather, it was a 'chant d'amour lascif'. It was an unrestrained orgy of sinfully seductive sounds, depravedly fascinating. . . . [12]

Flesch believed that Kreisler's greatest success was relatively long in coming because his intense style of playing was ahead of its time; and he pointed out that Kreisler used vibrato much more freely than his predecessors had done. Once the public became used to and even began to demand this type of sound, Kreisler was clearly to be considered its leading practitioner.* With maturity, says Flesch, Kreisler achieved a much more refined musical style while continuing to benefit from the gains he had made in tone production. 'The quality of his tone was unmistakable, incomparable and unequalled.' [13]

Flesch also considered Kreisler a great innovator in regard to the art of bowing:

Before him, we had the apparently unshakeable principle that the whole bow must be used whenever possible and at all costs. . . . Kreisler's example shows that grandeur and intensity are by no means tied up with the use of the 'whole bow'. He used the extreme point just as seldom as the extreme nut. . . . This bowing economy was counter-balanced by his characteristic bow pressure which, always slightly accentuated, was in its turn automatically regulated by his extraordinarily intensive vibrato. In his case, dynamics and shadings were effected much more by varied rationings of the length of stroke than by changes of the point of contact. [14]

Flesch considered some aspects of Kreisler's left-hand tech-

---

*It would be wrong, however, to assume, as many have done, that the frequent adoption of vibrato was the invention of Ysaÿe, Kreisler and their contemporaries. As early as 1749, Francesco Geminiani wrote of what he called the 'close shake' in his *A Treatise of Good Taste in the Art of Music*: '. . . you must press the finger strongly upon the string . . . and move the wrist in and out slowly and equally, when it is long continued, swelling the sound by degrees, drawing the bow nearer to the bridge, and ending it very strong, it may express majesty, dignity, etc. But making it shorter, lower and softer, it may denote affliction, fear, etc., and when it is made on short notes, it only contributes to make their sound more agreeable; and for this reason it should be made use of as often as possible.'

nique wanting, and blamed this on the latter's notorious dislike of practice and warm-up sessions:

It often happened that his finger technique was not altogether spotless; but this defect, to which one grew accustomed in time, could not weaken one's enjoyment of his playing to any appreciable extent. On the day of a concert he did not change his usual activities in the slightest, and on the platform he displayed an admirable sang-froid. [15]

Flesch concludes:

When all is said and done, Kreisler has been the most important figure for us violinists since Ysaÿe's decline; he has fundamentally influenced the development of our art as no other violinist of his time has done. In the history of violin playing he will live not only as an artist whose genius stimulated and expanded the art, but also as a most valuable symbol of a whole epoch. As a man, finally, despite his unheard-of success, he has remained simple and kind-hearted. [16]

Another competent observer of Kreisler's technique was Michael Raucheisen, who was his accompanist for nearly a dozen years. Raucheisen was a professional violinist and violist as well as pianist. He mentions that Kreisler kept the hair of the bow so taut that

no other violinist could play with it, but from that fact stems the purity of his tone, without auxiliary noises. . . . Shortly before a recital begins, he tunes his strings slightly higher than the tuning of the piano, in order that the flageolet tones and the open strings won't sound flat. I often admonish young violinists to tune their fiddles as sharp as possible, because gut strings always give when they become warm. . . . The psychological secret of Kreisler's imposing musicianship, his charm, personality and freshness lies in the multiplicity of his intellectual interests. . . . [27]

André Benoist, another of Kreisler's accompanists, commented:

He played with a golden tone and dazzling technique. At first sight, one wondered at his perfection, for his right elbow was raised high most of the time, contrary to the orthodox way most violinists are taught. But with him it was unimportant, for no matter how wrong it looked, it always sounded beautiful. [18]

Kreisler did not like to talk about technique. He would gladly discuss music itself or musical philosophy; but, like many outstanding artists, he was either unable or unwilling to explain how he played. When called upon to praise the benefits of diligent practising, he became even more diffident, and for obvious reasons. But Kreisler's statements about his own way-wardness in this area are undoubtedly exaggerated. We know, for instance, that his wife, in the early years of their marriage, forced him to practise for a certain period each day; and his accompanists, while admitting that Kreisler never practised the programmes which he was currently performing, report that he would carefully rehearse pieces scheduled for concerts three or four weeks in the future. This is not an uncommon method; nor was his custom of learning music by silently studying scores while travelling unusual. Many accomplished musicians prepare in this way: physical labour with the instrument is simply the second phase in the process of mastering a com-position. Finally, we have Rachmaninov's wry comment to the effect that his good friend Kreisler did not have to practise since he gave so many performances!

Kreisler was a fairly prolific composer, and many of his short pieces for the violin became highly popular as light programme-fillers. Some of these he published under his own name; others, written in imitation of earlier styles of composition, he passed off quite successfully and for a long time as works of composers from the distant past. Couperin's *Chanson Louis XIII*, Padre Martini's *Andantino*, Porpora's *Menuet* – these and many other ostensibly seventeenth- and eighteenth-century pieces were in fact written in the early twentieth century by Fritz Kreisler, and not merely arranged by him, as he originally claimed. Leafing through Grove's *Dictionary of Music and Musicians*, he had simply 'borrowed' the names of some dimly-remembered or altogether forgotten composers.

At first he told the curious that he had bought the manuscripts of these works for about $8000 from monks at a monastery in Avignon. This story was altered and manipulated over the years and according to the circumstances; many sceptical souls suspected what was going on, and some of Kreisler's friends knew for certain. ('What's Fritz doing?' Thibaud asked Harriet Kreisler one day. 'Oh, just writing some Pugnani,' she replied.) Clearly Kreisler greatly enjoyed the harmless and delightful little hoax he had perpetrated. Finally, in 1935, he revealed the truth. Most people – musicians, musicologists, critics and others – blushed at their own gullibility and accepted Kreisler's joke with good grace; but a few – most notably Ernest Newman – were incensed and severely castigated the violinist for what they considered to be his lack of seriousness. Kreisler defended himself and a great commotion ensued in the press; in the end, however, the innocuous little pieces remained in Kreisler's repertoire and in the repertoires of many of his colleagues. The only change was that his name appeared more often in concert programmes, while the names of Pugnani, Francoeur and others practically disappeared.

In 1903 Kreisler made his first recordings; eventually he became the highest-paid recording instrumentalist of his time. (Flesch states that between 1924 and 1930, for example, Kreisler's record royalties amounted to $175,000 per year; and evidence seems to support that statement.) We are fortunate that those recordings exist.

Kreisler's name has somehow come to symbolize sentimentality, *schmalz*, to many musicians too young to have heard him. The recordings he made are evidence enough that such notions are largely groundless. One outstanding example of Kreisler's art is the Beethoven Sonata in G Major, Op. 30 No. 3, in which he is partnered by Rachmaninov. The first movement, *Allegro assai*, is played with great lightness and with a wonderful warmth of tone; despite an occasional suggestion of rushing, the tempo is essentially very steady. After a slightly shaky beginning, the second movement, *Tempo di menuetto*, proceeds evenly. Kreisler's tone is unexaggeratedly sweet, his cadences gracefully simple; and he never loses his sense of forward motion. The last movement, *Allegro vivace*, is extraordinary: Kreisler's playing is both lyrical and buoyant, and all within the framework of an uncompromisingly quick tempo. There are no ugly sounds; and even the violin's accompanying figures are played with warmth.

In the recordings of the Beethoven and Mendelssohn concerti made with the Berlin State Opera Orchestra under the direction of Harry Blech in the 1920s we again hear great beauty of tone, supported by a firm concept of where the music is going. The Beethoven shows occasional fluctuations of tempo which seem excessive in comparison with common practice today; but they are reasoned and consistent, not arbitrary or haphazard. The intonation is not always perfect in the first movement, but there is great poise and grace to the playing. *Rubato* is frequently used, but in a controlled way and with an unerring sense of agogic contour. Some of Kreisler's bowings – *e.g.* the alternation of staccato and legato in bars 315 *et seq.* – seem old-fashioned

today. The second movement is calm and radiant, Kreisler's sound rich, seamless; and the Finale has a tremendous lilt to it. The Mendelssohn Concerto is a wonder of elegance and fleet-footedness, achieved above all through superb bowing, and with an overall sense of motion that is breathtaking. Kreisler re-recorded these concerti in London a decade later; but although the recorded sound is better than in the earlier versions, Kreisler's playing had already begun to lose some of its effervescence.

In some ways, the greatest surprise for us youngsters of the post-Kreisler era comes from his recordings of his own short pieces. We have all heard the melodies of *Caprice viennois*, *Tambourin chinois*, *Schön Rosmarin* and others many times; yet Kreisler's playing of them is a minor revelation. His use of *rubato* is of course continual, but it is in no way the sort of wilful, amorphous *rubato* which we have been taught to associate with traditional Viennese music-making. Kreisler's *rubato* is robust, precise; it brings verve and freshness to these lovely little pieces, rather than making them soggy and attenuated. The snap of the anticipated second beats in *Schön Rosmarin*, the quiet nostalgia of *Liebesleid* and the zest of *Liebesfreud* are a lesson well worth learning in musical rhetoric.

Discussing 'warmth' in an artist's playing is a dangerous activity; but the peculiarly warm quality of Kreisler's tone is so striking that it would be cowardly not to try to understand the phenomenon. Flesch approaches the subject by stating, apropos Kreisler's famous vibrato, that it was

ultimately but the inevitable result of his highly individual need for an increased intensity of expression. In any kind of artistic activity, it is always the impulse, the expressive need, the inner compulsion which dictates in the first place, and not the technical equipment. Just as a hungry man will always get hold of food, if need be by force, so every original artist finds, as a rule unconsciously, the necessary technical means to still his spiritual hunger. [19]

Flesch was writing in the 1930s. Elsewhere, he has written that to musicians of his generation, Kreisler's sound conveyed 'a sensuality intensified to the point of frenzy'.[20] The Kreisler vibrato, which was the primary element of his sensuous sound, has become a part of standard modern violin technique; but the frankness and innocence of that sensuousness were his and his alone. Several of today's violinists play with intensity and conviction equal to that of any of their predecessors whose work has come down to us through recordings; nevertheless, the quality of their sound is obviously and necessarily very different from Kreisler's. Musicians nowadays must attempt, in an age that has gone bad, to understand works of art of a bygone time. Even the greatest artists of today, however profound their vision may be, are re-discoverers, re-capturers, conservers. What astonishes us in Kreisler's playing is its open-eyed freshness, its inevitability. A few short decades after the close of his career, we cannot believe that life could ever have been the way his playing tells us it was.

Chapter Six

Pablo Casals

❖❖❖❖❖❖❖❖❖❖❖❖❖❖❖❖❖❖❖❖❖❖❖❖❖❖❖❖❖❖❖❖❖❖❖❖

KREISLER called Pablo Casals 'the greatest musician ever to draw a bow.' No instrumentalist in modern times has been more respected by his colleagues, more admired by his public, more esteemed by the non-musical world than Casals. No professional musical career has been as long as his (he was a paid choirboy at the age of five, gave his first public performance as a cellist at the age of twelve, and performed for the last time at the age of ninety-six); and no one has had as dramatic an influence on the technical approach to an instrument as he had on that of the cello. For although players of all instruments are heirs to a variety of methods and theories, there is not a cellist active today who is not a direct or indirect beneficiary of Casals' innovations. His moral authority was also great: he was not afraid to stand up in the name of a cause he espoused or to say no to those he opposed.

Casals lived so long and was such a vital figure to the very end of his life that all but the youngest of today's musicians remember something of his existence and achievement. Even those of us who were small children when he was in his seventies and eighties grew up hearing his name mentioned with special reverence; and we, like musicians of our parents', grandparents' and great-grandparents' generations, associate Casals' name with the cello in a special way – very similar to the Paganini–violin and Liszt–piano connections. And what could be more just? After all, in addition to liberating cello technique, Casals opened up new worlds of repertoire and brought to the instrument a dignity and popularity that it had not previously enjoyed.

Fuller-Maitland heard him in London at the turn of the century and said: 'I was long since convinced that [Alfredo] Piatti and [Robert] Hausmann had said the last word in violoncello-playing, but my eyes were opened when Casals came and played the unaccompanied C Major Suite of Bach. . . . Casals surpassed all violoncellists in my memory. . . .'[1]

It was not only the freedom of Casals' technique that

129

musicians like Fuller-Maitland, trained in the nineteenth century, found remarkable; it was his ability to draw the listener into the very heart of the music. This is a rare capacity in musicians of any age, for it presupposes a total immersion on the performer's part in the substance of the works he plays, and an endless attempt to reach a deeper understanding of them. Those works, according to Casals, were no longer to be to the virtuoso 'only the tragic and moving *mise-en-scène* for [his] feelings', as Liszt had said;[2] they were to be the Word, the source of all possibilities, the eternally-to-be-sought and eternally unobtainable goal. Casals, whose approach to his art was a religious one, said early in his career that a serious musician 'must seek the truth in simplicity and think only of the music'.[3] What this very telling statement means is that however difficult and however important it may be to come to grips with every detail of a composition, it is still more difficult and still more important to reassemble the results of one's search in a whole that is greater than the sum of its parts. If one does not resist the temptation to underline one's discoveries and to exaggerate their significance, one will be guilty of self-aggrandizement and of obscuring the sense of the music. To Casals, this attitude was at least as fundamental a factor in music-making as solid technique: it meant that from a moral point of view the means were even more important than the end.

The Casals phenomenon grew out of an unusual environment. Casals' father was a church organist in the town of Vendrell, Catalonia, Spain, where the future cellist was born on 29 December 1876. (His first name was Pau, the Catalan form of Paul; but professionally he generally used the Castillian form, Pablo, outside of Catalonia.) Carlos Casals also composed and taught piano and singing. From the age of four Pau studied the piano, which he adored and learned to play very well, and the rudiments of musical theory; and the following year he began to sing in his father's church choir. Somewhat later he was given lessons on the violin and the organ, and occasionally replaced his father at church services. He did not begin to study the cello until he was eleven – a rather advanced age for someone who was to become such a master; but of course his central nervous system would already have been well developed along the right lines through his earlier instrumental studies.

Pau's mother exerted a tremendous influence on him, and even at the end of his life he referred to her as the most extraordinary person he had ever known. Pilar Defilló was born in Puerto Rico of Catalan parents; her father and one of her brothers had committed suicide after having been tortured for activities against the Spanish regime on the island. She first came to Catalonia when she was eighteen, and it was there that she met and married Carlos Casals. According to her son, she was a hard-working, intelligent, outspoken woman who cared for neither the Spanish monarchy nor the Church, and who brought her children up to act according to their beliefs, whether that meant accepting the sacrifices of a musical career or – as in the case of Pau's younger brother, Enrique – going into exile to avoid military service. It was she who encouraged Pau to pursue his musical studies: her husband had initially wanted his son to become a carpenter; and it was she who insisted that the boy be allowed to study the cello at the Municipal School of Music in Barcelona. His teacher was Josep García, scion of the same family that had produced the singers Manuel García, Maria Malibran and Pauline Viardot. The boy earned money by playing in cafés.

Through the composer and pianist Isaac Albéniz, Casals was given an introduction to Count Guillermo de Morphy in Madrid. At seventeen the boy moved to the capital; and the Count, a highly skilled musician and a man of wide cultural interests, had a great influence on Casals' intellectual development. Furthermore, de Morphy saw to it that his young protégé was presented at court, where he quickly became a favourite. He continued his studies at the Madrid Conservatory and benefited particularly from his chamber music work and general musical discussions with the Conservatory's director, Jesús de Monasterio, whom he later referred to as the greatest musical influence on his life, excepting his father.

After a difficult sojourn in Brussels and Paris, Casals returned to Barcelona, where he began to do a great deal of teaching and orchestral playing. Then, in 1899, he made his first solo appearances in London (Crystal Palace) and Paris (Concerts Lamoureux), and his success was so great that his international career was launched. He was twenty-two years old; and for nearly three-quarters of a century he was to maintain his position as one of the most highly regarded performing musicians in the world.

Casals' technical innovations almost immediately earned him a place in the history of string playing. It appears that even as an adolescent beginner he had grasped the absurdity of cello

131

teaching as it then existed. Pupils were made to clasp books between upper arm and body in order to restrict movement. (The violin was also taught in this way, but the technique seems even more ridiculous when applied to the much bulkier cello.) Young cellists were also forced to adhere to rigidly traditional methods of fingering. Casals gave a great deal of thought to these and related problems; and when he began to perform internationally, the boldness of his playing and the success of his approach to the instrument caused progressive pedagogues to discard much of what they had previously accepted as immutable.

He determined, among other things, that the right arm should be used more freely, which allowed for more subtle control of the bow through the wrist. Connected with this was his determination not to use the whole length of the bow on every stroke – a common practice in the nineteenth century – but rather to vary the length of the stroke according to the requirements of the music. (Kreisler, as we know, was coming to a similar conclusion about violin technique at about the same time.) Casals himself said:

I find that whenever something seems to go against music it is reflected in an ugly and inelegant gesture; even in my childhood I felt awkward whenever I watched violinists or violoncellists using the whole bow all the time. It seemed useless to me. . . . It is quite natural to use it in all its length for long notes just as it is to use only part of it for shorter notes. The right hand should have the power to use whichever part of the bow is appropriate to the musical meaning of each note. . . .

In order to acquire the maximum of suppleness in the handling of the bow, the first thing and the most elementary is to hold it properly. One sees such curious things: only the other day as I was giving the first lesson to a new pupil, I noticed that he was holding his bow with all the fingers pointing to the right, which produced an unnecessary contortion of the wrist, bound to be tiring in the end. The bow must rest on the first joint and should press on the point of articulation of the first and second joint. In that position the hand is placed naturally and the wrist is free.[4]

Another of Casals' innovations was the use of what he called 'finger extensions', which meant stretching a finger of the left hand, when convenient, beyond the position in which the hand happened to be resting at a given moment, rather than shifting the entire hand. Casals determined that awkward shifting was 'detrimental to the music played'; and he denied that an unusually large hand was required for his method of finger extensions:

132

I have not an exceptional hand, but it is a flexible one which allows me these great extensions of finger. . . . If one's hands are too small it would be better to give up playing the cello. But with a normal hand a cellist should be able to include this extension of fingers in his technical equipment. These extensions should be practised in such a way that the maximum result can be attained with the least possible contraction of the muscles. In each case I choose the fingering which seems the simplest and the safest.[5]

Within a few years of his appearance on the international concert circuit, Casals' ideas were being adopted by thousands of colleagues, teachers and students around the world. By 1930 the British cellist and teacher Juliette Alvin was able to write in *The Musical Times*:

It cannot be too often repeated that Casals has wrought a revolution in cello playing. Having first discovered, probably by sheer instinct, new and hitherto unknown possibilities of unlimited scope for the cello, he then constructed a technique based on irrefragable logic and adaptable to any normal hand. . . . I have never found a pupil who, after having his left hand placed in the correct position, was not able to enjoy the extraordinary help given by Casals's fingering. . . . Hands, arms, the entire body, are used in a perfectly normal way. . . . Nothing is overlooked, not even the position of the feet, which is worked out to give comfort and stability to the body and to ensure an easy grasp of the instrument. . . .[6]

The effect of Casals' practical ideas impressed all string players – Flesch among them:

Casals's revolutionary influence on the development of cello playing is above all due to the fact that his technique permits him to play on this weighty and unwieldy instrument as on a violin. Despite his small hand, he renounced all dubious glissandos which served merely to surmount long distances in comfort, not to realize any expressive need. No more of the usual whining effeminacy in cantilenas, complete with intolerable noises during those runs (not to speak of double stoppings) which every listener fears; no more babies' howls in high positions. Here, for the first time, was uncompromising cello playing, a noble, masculine style in both cantilena passages and accompaniments requiring technical brilliance. . . .[7]

The Casals story continues along traditional lines: concerts, concerts and more concerts; friendships with noted musicians, other artists, elected and hereditary heads of state and other people of note; and above all a great deal of study and practice – for Casals was an assiduous worker. 'I give every moment I can to practice', he once said. 'I envy the fortunate ones who can dispense with it but, for myself, I cannot.'[8] He always suffered from nervousness before concerts, but his unshakeable technique and will power counterbalanced that state.

Casals made his first American tour as an assisting artist to soprano Emma Nevada in 1901–2; he returned for his first solo tour in 1904, playing for Theodore Roosevelt at the White House and later giving the first New York performance of Richard Strauss's *Don Quixote* at Carnegie Hall under the composer's direction. His American manager wanted Casals, who was already quite bald, to wear a toupee. Paderewski had by then set the style for long-haired, flamboyant musicians, and the serious little Catalan cellist did not satisfy romantic requirements. Casals refused; so the enterprising manager let the reason for Casals' premature baldness be known: the cellist had given a lock of his hair to each of the women he had loved!

In fact, it was only two years later that Casals became involved in one of the few serious love affairs of his life. From 1906 to 1912 he lived with his gifted but mercurial student, Guilhermina Suggia. He wanted to marry her, but she was afraid that marriage would destroy her career. (On the other hand she occasionally allowed herself to be billed in concert programmes as Mme P. Casals-Suggia.) Their years together appear to have been particularly difficult ones for Casals, who was a proud and jealous man. There was some equivocation in Suggia's relations with their mutual friend, the famed British musician and scholar Donald Francis Tovey; this caused Casals to break permanently with Suggia and temporarily with Tovey. In 1914 Casals married the American singer Susan Metcalfe. But as he himself said, their 'life together was not a happy one', and they separated in 1928.[9]

During the years before the First World War Casals made Paris his home, often undertaking joint recital tours with pianist Harold Bauer; and in 1905 he formed a trio with violinist Jacques Thibaud and pianist Alfred Cortot which eventually became one of the most celebrated chamber ensembles of the century. He was on friendly terms with many composers, including de Falla, Granados, Debussy, Ravel, d'Indy, Casella, Rimsky-Korsakov, Rachmaninov and Scriabin; and several other composer friends (e.g. Emanuel Moór, Tovey, Fauré and Schoenberg) wrote works for him to play. In addition to personal acquaintanceship with several generations of leading instrumentalists, he was friendly with the painters Degas, Carrière and Utrillo, the philosopher Henri Bergson, the writer Romain Rolland and the statesmen Georges Clemenceau and Aristide Briand. Casals had become one of the foremost musicians of the day. Edvard Grieg heard him and wrote of the experience: 'This man does not *perform*, he resurrects!' And Ysaÿe, after playing much chamber music and Brahms' Double Concerto with Casals in Russia in 1912, reported to his wife that his younger colleague was 'truly an artist, full of depth and feeling, extremely musical in the widest sense; not the slightest detail is neglected, all is brought out with tact, knowledge and discernment and without any posing or . . . any movement of the body. . . .'[10]

Casals taught a great deal, too, and most of the important cellists of the century passed his way sooner or later, some for extended instruction, others simply for assistance in resolving specific technical or musical problems. He helped to found and maintain the Ecole Normale de Musique in Paris and frequently gave lessons and master classes there.

With the substantial earnings from his concerts, Casals was able to buy himself a seaside villa at San Salvador, near his native Vendrell. He spent his holidays there, studying and enjoying pastimes like tennis, chess, dominoes, horseback-riding, swimming and hiking. But he certainly did not use his money entirely for selfish purposes. In 1920, for example, he founded and partially supported a new orchestra in Barcelona; and in so doing, he was able to merge personal ambition with public beneficence. He had long wanted to devote more of his time to conducting ('If I have been happy scratching away at a cello, how shall I feel when I can possess the greatest of all instruments – the orchestra?' he had written to his friend, the Dutch musician Julius Röntgen);[11] and at the same time, he was fired with the idea of raising the level of musical life in Catalonia. He put an enormous amount of effort into organizing the ensemble, but just before rehearsals were scheduled to begin, he fell violently ill. However, the first season of the Orquestra Pau Casals finally opened on 13 October 1920, with a programme of music by Bach, Beethoven, Ravel and Liszt.

Casals believed that the job of the conductor was above all to teach; and British pianist Harriet Cohen, who was a soloist under his direction, said that 'he and his orchestra were like chamber music players, all working unselfishly for the good of the composer, for the glory of music.'[12] Since Casals himself was subsidizing the orchestra, he could spend as much time as he liked polishing every detail of a score. To spend seven, eight or nine hours rehearsing one symphony was common practice in Barcelona. But when Casals guest-conducted orchestras with rigid schedules and limited rehearsal periods, the results were not always so successful. Bernard Shore, principal violist of the BBC Symphony Orchestra during the 1930s, was a great admirer of Casals the cellist and the musician; but he wrote of his conducting:

Unfortunately the orchestra often find it impossible to grasp what he is striving for, and at times wish to heaven he would play it on the 'cello. His stick would be reckoned quite efficient in an ordinary conductor, but it is inadequate to express that magnificent mind of his. Frequently it lets him down, being somewhat indefinite. When ensemble goes a little awry he flaps both arms violently, but without sufficient grip to draw together the ragged ends. The stick . . . is not always quite clear, and because of this the orchestra is never perfectly confident, particularly at the beginning of movements and at changes of tempi. . . . The orchestra needs something more than that he himself should be living in the music. . . .[13]

And Flesch recounted the tale that 'when a Viennese orchestral musician was asked, before a concert under Casals, what the latter was to conduct, he replied, "I'm sure I don't know what Casals is going to conduct. *We* are going to play the 'Pastoral' Symphony." '[14]

Nevertheless, the Orquestra Pau Casals was a great success; and in connection with it, Casals was able to fulfil another dream: he founded the Workingmen's Concert Association in Barcelona. Anyone whose income was under 500 pesetas (approximately £20 at that time) a month could join for the equivalent of 20 pence (one dollar) per year. Casals' orchestra played six concerts for the society every year, and he recalled the first such occasion, in the autumn of 1928:

More than two thousand workers crowded into the concert hall. When I looked at those rows of simply dressed men and women waiting for the concert to start, I felt an indescribable elation. At the end of the performance, the entire audience arose and gave the orchestra a thunderous ovation. Then they started chanting my name. Those shouts of the working people of Barcelona, I think, meant more to me than any applause I had ever received.[15]

136

20. Pablo Casals (1876–1973) changed commonly held notions about cello-playing even more radically than Kreisler had done for violin-playing. The boldness and success of his approach brought him international fame when he was still in his mid-twenties. By the time this photo was taken, during Casals' American tour of 1914–16, he had no serious rivals in the field.

21, 22. These two portraits show Casals in what can only be called his 'early' old age. He was in his seventies when they were taken, but he still had a quarter-century of playing, conducting and teaching ahead of him. Casals never stopped studying; he sought not only technical mastery, but also an understanding of every note in relation to every other note. As a protest against the fascist regime in his native Spain, he withdrew from regular concert activity in 1946 and never resumed it; but he did appear at festivals and on special occasions. (*Below*) Casals during a chamber music session. (*Opposite*) A striking image of an extraordinary master.

23. Wanda Landowska (1879–1959) was the first outstanding harpsichordist of the twentieth century. She dedicated most of her life to studying the music of the Baroque and earlier periods and to bringing the fruits of her efforts to the attention of an often uninterested musical world. Landowska's artistry, conviction and intelligence enabled her to demonstrate that what she was doing was of the highest artistic significance and to initiate an international revival of interest in early music. The photo (*above*) shows her seated at her custom-made Pleyel harpsichord in the late 1920s.

24, 25, 26. (*Opposite, above*) Landowska plays for Tolstoy at his estate, Yasnaya Polyana, in 1908. (*Below*) Both Manuel de Falla (*left*) and Francis Poulenc (*right*) composed works for Landowska – the former his Concerto for harpsichord, flute, oboe, clarinet, violin and cello (1923–6) and the latter his *Concert champêtre* (1927–8).

27. From 1941 onwards
Landowska lived in the
United States, first in New
York and then in Lakeville,
Connecticut. There she
continued to study and to
teach. She performed until
she was seventy-five and
made a series of important
recordings. Here she is seen
in Lakeville in 1948 with a
first edition copy of one book
of Couperin's *Pièces de
clavecin*.

28. Landowska in Lakeville, *c.* 1950. 'The most beautiful thing in the world', she said, 'is precisely the conjunction of learning and inspiration . . . I followed my vocation and never ceased to work without ever compromising.'

Eventually, the association numbered 300,000 members in all of Catalonia, published its own highly sophisticated musical journal and formed its own workers' orchestra. Casals was justifiably proud of his achievement. Indeed, he became so popular in Catalonia that when the Spanish Republic came into being in 1931, he became president of the Catalan Music Council, and he participated to a greater degree than ever before in the cultural life of his country. (Although he had been befriended and supported by several generations of the Spanish monarchy, his sentiments were always strongly republican, and he favoured a large measure of Catalan autonomy.)

It was also during his fifties and early sixties that Casals made the majority of his most important recordings. The American critic B. H. Haggin has written of Casals' recordings of the Bach Cello Suites: 'This is something you would almost not believe you had heard in a performance, after it was over; but you can put the needle back at the beginning of the Sarabande of No. 2 and find that it did happen; and there it is on the record for all time.'[16] Future generations of musicians will owe as much gratitude as we owe today to Fred Gaisberg and other record producers for having induced the reluctant cellist to make records. 'I was some years in coming to [financial] terms with Casals', reported Gaisberg, 'for the simple reason that, compared with the violin, 'cello records have not such a universal appeal and to submit to him terms that would approximate to those of Kreisler, Heifetz or Menuhin was not easy.'[17] In the end, Casals recorded a substantial portion of his repertoire; and Gaisberg, who was accustomed to microphone-shy string players and their complaints about the deleterious effects of humidity, was delighted to find that 'the most phlegmatic and casual of recorders was Casals who, I am sure, could extract golden tones even from a cigar-box strung in a monsoon. I have seen his only D-string break in the middle of recording a Brahms sonata. Nothing daunted, he would tie it up with a sailor's knot, relight his pipe and continue recording.'[18]

What is most striking in Casals' recordings is the conviction behind every phrase, every note he played. He once told Harriet Cohen: 'I practise as if I were going to live to be five hundred years old'[19] – which means not only that he strove for complete technical mastery, but that he studied every detail until he understood its position in relation to every other detail. It was not enough, he believed, to possess outstanding musical

145

instincts or to be able to depend upon an incomparable technique. On the contrary: those were points of departure. Gaisberg compares Casals as an interpretative executant to Toscanini; and one may recall the latter's statement to the effect that the two faults he could not excuse in his fellow-musicians were negligence and laziness, because they were the opposite of love and faith. Life is not easy for the artist who feels so great a responsibility and who sets himself such standards; and this explains one of the stories Casals most often told about himself. When he was twenty-five his left hand was injured by a falling rock during a mountain-climbing expedition in California. His first thought was, 'Thank God, I'll never have to play the cello again!'[20] Despite all the success his work brought him, it was also a form of servitude and of eternal dissatisfaction.

But the results of some of his efforts can be heard today; and any discussion of his recordings must begin with the Bach Unaccompanied Suites, which Gaisberg 'persistently worried him into recording' between 1936 and 1939.[21] Casals was the first person to play these works in concert, and he was extraordinarily devoted to them – even by his standards. One may legitimately argue with some of his 'unauthentic' (for Baroque-period music) bowings or with some occasionally explosive dynamics; but one feels a bit ridiculous in doing so – as if one were standing in front of a mountain and shaking a finger at its unevenness. By the time these recordings were made, Casals had been tenaciously and lovingly studying the suites for half a century; and it is therefore no surprise that one is immediately impressed by the naturalness and ease of his playing of them. In the Third Suite (C major), for instance, the Prelude flows beautifully and lightly; the Allemande demonstrates a wonderful grasp of phrasing and an equally wonderful rhetorical sense; the Courante is conceived as a sort of dialogue between a high voice and a low one; the Sarabande's dignified singing line is sustained almost beyond belief; the Bourrées are vital but always graceful; and the Gigue – most remarkable of all – is played with unrestrained high spirits and without a hint of caution. The whole Suite, in fact, sounds completely free. Casals gives a very dramatic reading to the Fifth Suite (C minor) – the one in which the top string is tuned to G instead of A. Although the Courante is taken at so fast a tempo that its cadences seem abrupt, the other movements are completely convincing and have a rare and unmistakable feeling of inevitability about them; and in the last three sections in particular (Sarabande, Gavottes and Gigue) Casals creates an amazing and unanticipated cumulative effect.

His recordings of the Beethoven Sonatas for cello and piano are characterized above all by their vocal emphasis. There is not a note, however short, that has not been both endowed with a melodic importance of its own and conceived as part of a larger melodic unit. At times, this emphasis causes a movement to lose its shape. For example, in the Fifth Sonata (D major, Op. 102 No. 2), which Casals recorded with Mieczysław Horszowski in 1939, he gives the principal theme a wonderful feeling of restrained power; and the development section and coda are played intensely, almost mysteriously. But the second theme is so expansive that it comes close to bursting. Casals begins the second movement at an exceedingly slow tempo, which he begins to push by the time he reaches the fifth bar, and which he has increased considerably by the time he reaches the D major section. When he has an accompanying figure, as in bars 34–6, he plays too loudly; and throughout the ending of the movement the pushings and pullings of tempo seem excessive. (Poor Horszowski has his hands full trying to follow Casals' meanderings here. This brings to mind a statement by Sir Adrian Boult, a great Casals admirer who, however, warned: 'There is no known conducting technique for keeping an orchestra together with this man! The only useful practice would be fly-swatting.')[22] The third movement is also played at a rather sedate tempo, which makes the graceful parts sound pretty and the dramatic parts ponderous. Casals' recording of the first Beethoven Sonata (F major, Op. 5 No. 1) with Rudolf Serkin (1953) is even more puzzling: the Allegro section of the first movement is heavy, its effects exaggerated, and generally very uneven; and the second movement, too, is often too emphatic.

It is a great relief to hear his performance of Beethoven's 'Archduke' Trio (B-flat major, Op. 97), recorded with Thibaud and Cortot in 1928 – although Cortot often destroys the wonderful unity achieved by Thibaud and Casals. The first movement is played with great breadth, and fussy phrasing is avoided. The pizzicati in the development section are particularly exhilarating. Casals begins the second movement with a wonderful combination of lightness, warmth and humour, all of which are echoed by Thibaud but ruined by Cortot, who accelerates his solo parts, makes abrupt cadences and plays far too many wrong notes. The third movement comes off with simplicity and

147

intensity, as required; and Casals' phrasing, here as elsewhere, is of an extraordinarily vocal quality. The coda must be heard to be believed. The last movement is all pulsation and vitality – even the little repeated notes in the accompaniment.

All of Casals' musical and politico-cultural activities came to a temporary end with the disastrous outcome of the Spanish Civil War. He had worked hard for the Republican cause. Gaisberg saw him in the middle of that nightmarish period in his life. Casals was to visit Prague (April 1937) to perform the Dvořák Cello Concerto with George Szell and the Czech Philharmonic, and Gaisberg made arrangements to record the work the day after the concert.

Casals flew from Barcelona, arriving more dead than alive, but full of hope for a Republican victory in Spain. . . . The dress rehearsal and concert before packed houses were a huge success. Casals's *élan and stamina* kept him going for the whole of the next day when over twelve unsurpassed [78 r.p.m.] records were made, and then the little man collapsed, every ounce of his strength exhausted. . . .[23]

Casals' life was in danger as Franco's forces moved into Barcelona. (One of Franco's principal aides had 'joked' on the radio that if Casals were caught, his arms would be cut off at the elbow.) In the end, he fled across the border to the French town of Prades, thereafter doing whatever he could for his fellow Catalan refugees who were living in camps in the area. Within a few months the Second World War had begun, making life even more difficult for Casals and his compatriots. The German occupation was a particularly horrifying time for him, as for so many others; but he was left unmolested, and even managed to give a few concerts in neutral Switzerland.

At the end of the war he immediately resumed regular concert activity, with greater success than ever before. He had become a symbol of anti-fascist resistance, and his popularity in Britain, France and elsewhere reached its zenith. But when he realized that the Allies were not going to remove the Spanish Fascists from power, he made the most difficult decision of his life: he determined not to play again in public 'until the democracies changed their attitude toward Spain'.[24]

This is the moment to refer to two autobiographical books which were published with Casals' approval during his lifetime:

J. M. Corredor's *Conversations with Casals*, dating from the mid-1950s, and *Joys and Sorrows*, by Casals himself 'as told to' Albert E. Kahn in the late 1960s. (The latter book makes use of much material from the former.) One comes away from both of these works with mixed feelings. On the one hand, they reveal something of the functioning of the mind of this great instinctive musician; on the other, they do undeniably give the impression that Casals in his old age believed in his own sainthood. However much one may revere him, one must accept the fact that there were noteworthy inconsistencies in his actions; and the Spanish protest is one example. In Corredor's book, Casals states that in 1946 'I declared I would not accept any invitation or engagement from anywhere, as long as a free *regime*, based on the freedom and the will of the people, was not re-established in Spain.'[25] And he later mentioned that when asked to participate in a Belgian concert honouring the memory of his late friend and colleague Ysaÿe, he said: 'No, I cannot! There should not be an exception in my attitude, otherwise the situation would become impossible.'[26] But he did make exceptions. In 1950 an annual Bach festival was initiated at Prades, with Casals' performances programmed as its main attraction. A few years later he became the principal figure in Puerto Rico's Festival Casals. And later still he began to participate each summer in the Marlboro Festival in Vermont. In 1951 he conducted a concert in Zurich honouring his own seventy-fifth birthday; he conducted performances of his oratorio *El pessebre* (The Manger) – dedicated to world peace – on four continents; and there was the famous recital at the White House in 1961 when he played before President Kennedy, whose government's continuing economic support of Franco was one of the greatest factors in maintaining the Fascist regime in Spain. Casals would have said, and did indeed say, that these performances were all outside the mainstream of international concert activity, and that their purpose was entirely to promote world peace and greater understanding of the Spanish situation. Yet surely he realized that some of his actions – particularly the White House recital and the embrace he exchanged with Kennedy – puzzled many who had come to regard his attitude as uncompromising.

It would be absurd and petty to criticize a great performer for desiring to perform and for wanting to be appreciated. I for one am glad that Casals was able and willing to do as much as he did in his last years. I believe that he was sincere and spontaneous in

149

his deeds. But since we have so often been told that the façade, at least, was flawless, I feel obliged to point out that it was not.

Similarly, although Casals was a generous man, his attitude towards money was not entirely other-worldly. Gaisberg mentioned that he 'has always held out for the highest fee', but added that 'this is not because he is mercenary, but purely as a matter of prestige, so dear to the heart of a Catalan.'[27]

Casals may not have been self-righteous, but the Corredor and Kahn books – which contain much fascinating information – make him seem so. In that sense they do him a disservice. The sad fact is that one can discuss one's own humility only so long without arousing suspicion in one's listeners. Still, when one thinks of the sheer greed and stinginess of so many top-ranking artists, and of their utter unconsciousness of anything beyond the ends of their instruments, Casals' star shines very brightly indeed, and the cracks in his philosophy and discrepancies in his behaviour are easily passed over.

In 1955 Casals' devoted friend and housekeeper, Frasquita Vidal Puig de Capdevila, became gravely ill; and as she lay on her deathbed in Prades, Casals married her. Because of a solemn vow he had made to her, he accompanied her coffin to Spain (Vendrell and San Salvador) for the funeral and burial. This was his only return to native soil during the nearly thirty-five years between the fall of Barcelona and his death. Then, in 1957, the eighty-year-old cellist surprised many people by marrying his very young pupil Marta Montañez y Martinez. 'I was aware at the time', he remarked with amusement several years later, 'that some people noted a certain discrepancy in our ages – a bride-groom of course is not usually thirty years older than his father-in-law. . . .'[28] But he also spoke very movingly of his marriage:

Marta is the great love of my whole life, the only true love. She fills everything in me and has made up for all the emptiness of my life. Nothing can be compared to our perfect love and our ideal life together. It is a feeling I had never experienced before. I had never been happy. I found real happiness only with Marta.[29]

Casals continued to perform and teach all over the world throughout the 1960s and into the 1970s. In his mid-nineties he still began each day as he had been doing for the previous eighty years: he went to the piano and played two preludes and fugues from Bach's *Well-Tempered Clavier*.

150

I cannot think of doing otherwise. It is a sort of benediction on the house. But that is not its only meaning for me. It is a rediscovery of the world of which I have the joy of being a part. It fills me with awareness of the wonder of life, with a feeling of the incredible marvel of being a human being. The music is never the same for me, never. Each day it is something new, fantastic and unbelievable. That is Bach, like nature, a miracle!'[30]

It is often true of outstanding musicians when they become old that their greatest virtues degenerate, through exaggeration, into vices. Casals' most amazing quality was his ability to enliven every note he played – to give every note sense and direction. There were no lacunae in his playing, no passages rippled off for effect. He must have been a terribly obstinate man, because in his playing one can hear that he has wrestled with phrase after phrase, allowing nothing to elude his attention or to go unresolved. The material has submitted after a great struggle and its treasures are presented to us naturally, triumphantly, joyously. If in some of his recordings (the Beethoven Sonatas, for example, or the Schubert Quintet in which he is partnered by the Végh Quartet) one feels that too much juice has been pressed from each bar and that the overall structure has suffered as a result, the effort itself moves and instructs nonetheless: it tells us unequivocally that we must believe in and abandon ourselves to what we do if we wish to produce anything worthwhile. Nietzsche advised thinkers to 'write with blood, and you will find that blood will become spirit'. Casals, in his field, continues to represent precisely that sort of intense, all-embracing commitment to artistic expression.

Chapter Seven

Wanda Landowska

❖❖❖❖❖❖❖❖❖❖❖❖❖❖❖❖❖❖❖❖❖❖❖❖❖❖❖❖❖❖❖❖❖❖

I really don't know what I am doing among [professional virtuosi]; I have no contact with them. They are on their guard with me, thinking that I am a 'learned' musician. But I, aware of the little I know, feel ill at ease with them. For this reason, I live apart. They take it for aloofness.[1]

Wanda Landowska

LOOK AT A LIST of current musical events in London, New York, Paris, Milan, Vienna or any other major musical centre: nearly every night of the week, along with symphonic concerts, operas and piano and violin recitals, there are performances by groups with names like 'Musica Antiqua', 'Musicus Concentus', 'Baroque Players', 'Renaissance Consort' and the like. They play on harpsichords, clavichords, virginals, viols, rebecs, sackbuts, recorders, cornetts and a variety of other instruments which a generation ago were rarities in the concert hall. One of the most remarkable musical phenomena of our time has been this flowering of interest in early music and in the search for authentic styles of performing it.

No one person can take all the credit for this situation; but if there is one who deserves a larger share of the credit than anyone else, that person is Wanda Landowska. From the first decade of this century until her death in 1959, this woman dedicated herself with enormous energy to understanding the music of the past and to sharing the fruits of her efforts with an often uninterested musical world. She rediscovered music which had remained unplayed for centuries, brought to light equally for-gotten treatises which taught her something about how that music was to be approached, embroiled herself in decades of polemical combat in order to justify her work, became an expert in a number of related fields, taught, lectured, wrote books and articles and, above all, brought her brilliant interpretations to audiences throughout Europe and America. Her sense of purpose and of her own destiny was so strong that she was able to level all the obstacles in her path; consequently, the results of her struggle have no parallel in the history of music.

Nowadays, the early music camp contains – along with some truly gifted individuals – a number of demi-celebrities who perform like musicologists and theorize like performers. Landowska, a woman of great musicality, formidable technique and hard-won erudition, was a supremely gifted keyboard artist and a convincing propagandist who made certain that her arguments were ironclad before she put them forward. To those for whom her name is today associated in a vague way with the Baroque revival – to those, that is, who are not familiar with her recordings or writings – it may come as a surprise to hear her classified as a virtuoso. Liszt and Rubinstein were still very much alive when she was born (Warsaw, 5 July 1879) and Paderewski's career had not yet begun. Although she enjoyed poking fun at the stereotyped virtuoso, she herself would not have dreamt of beginning a recital without first establishing the proper atmosphere: the lighting on stage had to be very dim before she would glide, wraith-like, onto the platform, hands clasped as if in prayer and eyes cast heavenward. It is true that there was a great difference between Paganini dazzling his audiences by playing left-hand pizzicato trills in his Variations on *God Save the King* and Landowska subduing her public through her intense commitment to Bach's 'Goldberg' Variations; but the will to dominate the listener was similar.

Landowska was born into a musical family. Her father, a lawyer, and her mother, a linguist, were Polish Jews who had converted to Catholicism; and both were gifted amateur musicians. Even well-known figures like the baritone Mattia Battistini attended the Landowskis' musical gatherings. Wanda was very fond of her parents, and often spoke of her mother's generosity. 'She was unable to savour fruit or anything else alone. I shall never forget her gesture when she was saying, "Taste this apple!" She gave it all. I am only a feeble echo of my mother. . . . When I play a sarabande of Chambonnières, I wish to call out, "Come, help me bear this burden of love, this flame!" '[2]

It is not surprising that Landowska, like many a musical child growing up in Warsaw in the last century, should have been taught by Chopin specialists. Nevertheless, her first piano teacher, Jan Kleczyński, was a musician of broad outlook and, in Landowska's words, 'a kind and indulgent man' who allowed her 'to browse freely in the music which pleased me; and what pleased and fascinated me particularly was the music of former

154

times.'[3] Once, a woman who had been a pupil of Liszt came to the Landowski house and played some bravura pieces; then 'she attacked a piece that I did not know. Its rhythm and melodic outline struck me. The purity of the motive reminded me of some popular dance. . . . The woman stood and said, "*Le Tambourin* of Rameau". Every time I have played this *Tambourin* since, I have recalled my delight when I first heard it so many years ago!'[4]

Wanda's musical instruction began when she was four. She was gifted but undisciplined, and Kleczyński and the teachers who succeeded him often did not know how to deal with her. She resisted technical exercises and formal theoretical studies, and she insisted on playing more Bach than was considered healthy in those days. When she was fourteen Artur Nikisch, the great conductor, heard her play a Prelude and Fugue from *The Well-Tempered Clavier* and nicknamed her 'the Bacchante'. Two years later she was sent to Berlin to study composition with the same Heinrich Urban who had taught Paderewski and other well-known musicians. There she remained until the age of twenty-one, when she eloped to Paris with Henry Lew, a Polish Zionist and expert on Jewish folklore. She began to appear as a pianist, and some of her compositions were occasionally performed.

From the very start of her performing career, she included the music of Bach and other Baroque composers in her programmes. In fact, she seems to have had a sense of her mission from the time she was a small child, for she decided even then that someday she would play an entire programme of music by Bach, Mozart, Rameau and Haydn. 'I wrote this neatly on a sheet of paper decorated with Christmas pictures and sealed it in an envelope, on which I inscribed, "To be opened when I am grown up." '[5] As a young woman beginning to make her way as a concert artist, she played Baroque music on the piano: it was difficult enough to convince audiences to accept even that! Just as Casals astonished listeners at that time by playing an entire unaccompanied Bach Cello Suite in concert, the situation was no different in regard to Baroque repertoire for other instruments. It was considered charming and acceptable to insert a little piece like Rameau's *Le Tambourin* into a piano recital, as the Liszt pupil had done at the Landowski home. No one, however, with the exception of Anton Rubinstein, would have dreamt of doing an entire programme of pre-nineteenth-century music; and few apart from Rubinstein would have conceived of playing the keyboard music of any period on any instrument other than the piano. Even he did not have the means for doing so at his disposal; but in *Music and its Masters* (1892) he wrote:

I believe that the instruments of all times must have had tone-colouring and effects that we cannot produce on the pianoforte of today; that the compositions were always intended for the character of the instrument in use, and only upon such could be heard fully as intended – and so played upon the pianoforte of today would perhaps be heard to disadvantage. . . . We can, at any rate, know nothing definite of the instruments of that day; even those to be found in the museums of London, Paris, Brussels, etc., give us no idea, since time would destroy the tone of a pianoforte [sic] entirely beyond recognition, and, besides, to us the most important part, *the manner of playing these instruments*, is wholly unknown. It is strange how little the professional instrument-makers know of these things! . . . I cannot dismiss the idea that [Bach's harpsichord] must have had attachments that made it possible to vary the quality of tone, hence this desire for *registering* whenever I play these compositions. . . .[6]

Slowly, Landowska began to conclude that one could only satisfactorily play the music of the past on the instruments for which it was written. In 1889 the Pleyel piano factory in Paris had constructed a small harpsichord – a wooden-framed instrument based loosely upon eighteenth-century models. Landowska obtained one of these not long after her arrival in France; and by 1903 she had begun, hesitantly, to play a few short pieces on the harpsichord during her piano recitals. Today it may appear to us that she proceeded with excessive caution; but such was the level of ignorance among her contemporaries that she could not have chosen a different path. In 1905 the critic of the *Corriere della Sera*, reviewing Landowska's début in Milan, a musically sophisticated city, felt it necessary to explain to his readers what a harpsichord was and at what period in musical history it had been used. With near wonderment he emphasized that her performance was important not only as a curiosity, but also as an artistic event.

His comment is a revealing one. Thousands of mediocre players might have dragged harpsichords all over the world without helping this particular cause; but Landowska had the artistry, intelligence and conviction to demonstrate that what she was doing was not just for the sake of novelty, not mere frivolity, but rather something of the highest artistic significance. Bach, Couperin, Scarlatti and dozens of others were not simply historical figures: they were masters as accomplished in the musical languages of their times as Beethoven, Chopin and Wagner were accomplished in the musical languages of the nineteenth century. One does not make qualitative chronological differentiations in the visual arts or in literature – one does not say that painting in Cézanne's time was better than in Rembrandt's, or that writing in Flaubert's time was better than in Shakespeare's; so why say that musical composition in Brahms' day was better than in Couperin's?

This seems obvious to us today, but it was not so eighty years ago. Landowska and Lew decided to publish a work on Baroque and earlier music which would be both scholarly and polemical; and their book, *Musique Ancienne*, appeared in 1909. Music, it said, is progressive only in as much as its language changes with the passage of time. It is not progressive qualitatively – each period is not an improvement upon the last, but merely a change from the last.

Lew, an intelligent man and a scholar who did not mind a fight, was of great assistance to Landowska in regard to the methodology and presentation of the book; but her knowledge of the subject must already have been encyclopaedic. Keyboard specialist Howard Schott has written:

The depth of research that underlay *Musique Ancienne* can scarcely be grasped until one begins to catalogue all the source material quoted in the book. How many of her contemporaries who challenged Landowska had heard of, let alone read Jean Denis' *Traité de l'accord de l'espinette* (1650) or the *Lettre de Mr le Gallois à Mademoiselle Regnault de Solier* (1680)? In the days before microfilm and instant photocopies how many hours must this woman of astounding erudition and energy have spent in writing out extensive quotations from old treatises, in copying out rare early music, in studying, playing and thinking? Landowska even carried out research while touring. A musical supplement to the 15 April 1909 issue of *Le Monde Musical*, for instance, contains the first printing of the famous 'Nightingale' from Elizabeth Rogers' Virginal Book, 'from a copy furnished by Wanda Landowska', no doubt a by-product of her British tour of 1905. . . .[7]

It was difficult to make headway in the beginning, but Landowska managed to attract the attention and interest even of Rodin, Tolstoy – to whose estate at Yasnaya Polyana she twice (1907 and 1909) took her harpsichord – and other leading artists and men of letters. Strangely enough, many of the musicians most enthusiastic about the revival of early music (and it would be wrong to think that Landowska was alone in that enthusiasm) tried to discourage her from performing on the harpsichord. Some of them felt that the question of authentic instruments would only complicate the movement as a whole, while others simply did not like the sound of the harpsichord. But she persevered. One early and important supporter was Albert Schweitzer who, in his celebrated book on Bach, wrote in 1905: 'Anyone who has heard Wanda Landowska play the *Italian Concerto* on her wonderful Pleyel harpsichord finds it hard to understand how it could ever be played on a modern piano.'[8]

By 1912 Landowska had persuaded Pleyel to build a different type of harpsichord to her specifications. In many respects, this instrument was further from the authentic harpsichords of the past than the 1889 model had been. It had a sixteen-foot register in addition to its eight-foot and four-foot registers (most older instruments had only eight-foot or eight- and four-foot registers)*; changes in registration were controlled by pedals, rather than manually-operated levers; and the size and dip of its keys were closer to those of a piano than to those of an authentic harpsichord. There were other important differences besides. A pre-nineteenth-century harpsichord has a thin soundboard and light case, so that the plectra which pluck the strings may be very thin and still produce great resonance. In a heavy instrument like Landowska's Pleyel, with its less resonant soundboard, most of the sound must be produced by the strings, which must therefore be displaced by larger, thicker plectra. Furthermore, Landowska's harpsichord's plectra were made of leather rather than quill, with a resultantly duller sound.

Landowska claimed to have based her hand position and fingering on Couperin's *L'Art de toucher le clavecin*, but today's harpsichordists would argue that her techniques were more closely related to modern piano methods than to the practices described by sixteenth-, seventeenth- and eighteenth-century harpsichordists. She even insisted that her piano-trained students continue to practise technical exercises (including those created for the piano by Hanon, Tausig and others) on both the

---

*An eight-foot register sounds at the pitch indicated in the music· a sixteen-foot register sounds an octave lower than indicated; a four-foot register sounds an octave higher than indicated.

piano and the harpsichord. Fingers were to be kept tightly curved at all joints, and the keys were to be attacked in a way that would produce a wooden sound on an historical harpsichord. The sort of fingering adopted by Landowska (frequent passing of the thumb under other fingers, etc.) would have been inconvenient on an authentic harpsichord keyboard, for the simple reason that its keys are shorter than a piano's , and the thumb, therefore, has a harder time than the other fingers, particularly in rapid scale passages.

Because the Pleyel had pedals for changes of registration, Landowska was able to achieve brilliant, virtuosic changes in register which were not available to harpsichordists of the past and which are, consequently, regarded as wrong by today's players. Where it is inconvenient to pause to engage a stop manually, it is generally considered to be unnecessary to do so. Landowska's perception of the harpsichord as an instrumental ensemble in itself (trumpets, musettes, flutes, oboes, strings, harps, lutes, organ) was absolutely correct; but no individual old instrument was capable of producing such an enormous array of effects.

All of the above information is given by way of explanation and is in no way intended as a criticism of Landowska's approach. Had she not been a great musician, one would excuse her by saying that she was a pioneer; but in fact, she was both a pioneer and a great musician. As such, her grasp of and ability to convey the musical image were the most significant aspects of her work, and the instrument and techniques she employed to realize her intentions were of secondary importance. No excuses are required.

In 1913 Landowska instituted a harpsichord class at Berlin's Hochschule für Musik at the invitation of its director, Hermann Kretzschmar. But with the outbreak of the First World War the following year, both she and Lew, officially enemy aliens, had their passports taken away and were not allowed to leave Berlin. Landowska continued to teach through the war years, and the couple led a relatively happy if unconventional life: Lew's mistress shared their home with them. Shortly after the armistice was signed Landowska and her husband decided to return to France. Lew, however, was killed in an automobile accident, and his widow, now nearly forty, went back to Paris alone. Reduced nearly to penury, she soon resumed her concert tours and teaching activities. During the 1920s she made four trips to the

United States, usually with no fewer than four of her Pleyels in tow. She began to be in great demand, even touring as far afield as South America and Egypt. The battle was turning in her favour. Landowska even induced Pleyel to add an iron frame to her harpsichords, so that they would be more resistant to climatic changes.

The economic benefits of her new success enabled her to buy a home at Saint-Leu-la-Forêt, outside of Paris, and to establish there a school of early music. Her enormous library and her collection of antique and modern instruments were installed at Saint-Leu, and she regularly gave recitals in the concert hall which she had had built in the garden. One of the most noteworthy events of those years was the first complete public performance in modern times of Bach's 'Goldberg' Variations in May 1933. Her programmes at Saint-Leu were in general more challenging than those she dared offer to the mass public she played to on tour; and among the pupils who came to study with her were Ralph Kirkpatrick, Ruggero Gerlin, Clifford Curzon, Eta Harich-Schneider, Lucille Wallace, Putnam Aldrich and Aimée Van de Wiele.

Although Landowska had made some piano rolls in 1905 and some acoustical recordings during the 1920s, the greatest part of her discography was recorded from the 1930s onwards, first in France and then in the United States. I find some of the Parisian recordings to be the most wonderful documentations we have of her artistry. The brilliant characterization of the Scarlatti sonatas, the splendour and vitality of the Handel suites, make these albums landmarks in the history of the gramophone. Above all, Bach's Chromatic Fantasy and Fugue, recorded at Saint-Leu in 1935, demonstrates that one of the great musical minds of our time was in operation.

What is strange about that particular recording is that although Landowska does many things which most musicians today would regard as objectionable in the interpretation of Bach's music (excessive changing of registers, 'romantic' underlinings and the like), her grip on the material is so strong, her involvement so complete, that one cannot help but be carried along by the force of her playing. A great performance can only be produced by a musician who has an absolutely coherent vision of a work, an intense desire to share that vision, and the technical resources to realize it. There is moreover something about the very first bars of such a performance that pulls one into what is to follow. Stylistic quibbles, although important, must be cast aside in the face of such overwhelming conviction and excellence.

Another of Landowska's best-known French recordings is her Couperin album (1934). Many of the pieces it contains sound ponderous as she conceives them; yet, again, one must admire her complete immersion in what she sees to be the nature of each of them.

As the German army approached Paris in the spring of 1940, Landowska was forced to abandon Saint-Leu. She and Denise Restout, her student and companion, fled to Banyuls-sur-Mer in the south of France; but when life in the Vichy Republic became impossible for them, they embarked for the United States, where they arrived on 7 December 1941 – the day of the Japanese attack on Pearl Harbor. Once again, Landowska had been forced to uproot her existence. Now sixty-two, she had lost her home and all the treasures it contained, for the Nazis had done a very efficient job of looting the house at Saint-Leu. On 21 February 1942, two-and-a-half months after her arrival in New York, she appeared at Town Hall playing the 'Goldberg' Variations. She was received with tremendous enthusiasm. The last phase of her career had begun. She performed, gave master classes and began to record again.

The American recordings have a different sound from the earlier European ones. For the French engineers, the ideal seems to have been to approximate what a listener in a small hall would have heard, while the Americans appear to have wanted to make the listener feel that his head was inside the harpsichord. Given the Pleyel's complicated and noisy mechanism, this latter technique sometimes contributed an unpleasant, strident quality to the recordings. Nevertheless, many Landowska performances, particularly from her Bach repertoire, were successfully preserved – the Inventions, the 'Goldberg' Variations (which she had also recorded in France), the complete *Well-Tempered Clavier* and so on. The American edition of the 'Goldbergs' sold 35,000 copies in its first six years in the record shops[9] – an extraordinary figure for what was then considered to be a very esoteric piece of music.

A characteristic Landowska recording of this period is Bach's Prelude, Fugue and Allegro in E-flat major. This piece is often conceived as a unit to be played rather evenly – gently – throughout. Played well, there is a beautiful melancholy to this sort of

161

conception. Landowska, however, is not content with such a procedure. For her, the piece is a complex drama. The Prelude begins sternly, and only after building to a climax does it relax into the sweeter tone which most players adopt from the beginning. The Fugue, too, she plays severely. Because she does not break her chords, there is a certain heaviness to the playing. On the other hand, she stresses the harmonies, makes them expressive. The cadential passage at the end of the repetition of the Fugue is extremely rhetorical. In fact, if there is one single element that most musicians today would object to in Landowska's playing, it is her massive preparations of cadences, which sometimes seem to destroy the music's momentum. But after her solemn ending of the Fugue, she breaks into a very fast tempo for the Allegro and plays it brilliantly right to the end. This work was written for the *Lautenwerk* or lute-harpsichord, which Landowska herself describes as 'a harpsichord with gut strings introduced for the purpose of imitating the sonority of the lute and the theorbo'.[10] The piece therefore can be and often is played to beautiful effect as a circular and introspective lute-like work; but Landowska plays it, to equally beautiful effect, in the dialectical style of a sonata.

When the war ended Landowska wished to return to Saint-Leu; but her economic situation and advancing years made such a decision impossible. In 1947 she moved from New York to a house in Lakeville, Connecticut. Some of the items which the Nazis had pillaged from Saint-Leu found their way back to her.

Most of her time was occupied, as always, with study, practice and writing. Between 1950 and 1954 she devoted a great deal of energy to what she called her last will and testament – a complete recording of Bach's *Well-Tempered Clavier*. Once every few weeks, a crew of RCA technicians would arrive at Lakeville, set up their equipment in her living-room and remain in the area for two or three days to record, painstakingly, some of the forty-eight preludes and fugues which are the cornerstone of the keyboard literature. Then they would pack up and return to New York until Landowska was ready for the next session. She was seventy-five when she completed the task; and that same year she gave her last public performance – a recital at the Frick Museum in New York. Nevertheless, she continued to study, to teach (Rafael Puyana was one of her students in America) and even to record until shortly before her death, which occurred on 16 August 1959, a few weeks after her eightieth birthday.

Landowska felt that she had been given an important mission to fulfil in life; and as is often the case with prophets, she could be a difficult person. She did not take kindly to opposition. 'You play Bach your way', she is reported to have said to a performer who had differed with one of her interpretations, 'and I shall play him *his* way.' She was also capable of behaving badly towards her pupils. Schott was told that she once scheduled a performance in Berlin of a Bach concerto shortly before a young woman whom she had coached in the same work was due to play it in her Berlin début concert, 'thus demolishing', as Schott says, 'the pupil's chances of scoring a great success'. (Denise Restout claims that this story was the fabrication of a jealous and frustrated person.) He also characterizes her as 'acutely sensitive, authoritarian and chronically insomniac'[11] – all of which, of course, must have made regular contact with her difficult for those who did not adapt accordingly.

But it is clear that Landowska was a very wise person with a strong sense of humour (I understand that she particularly enjoyed risqué jokes), and someone who was willing to share everything she knew and experienced with those whom she liked. To a pupil who returned to her in 1950 after a ten-year absence and then reproached her for having changed her mind about much of what she had taught in the past, she wrote a very touching letter revealing both her wounded feelings and her contempt for the pupil's obtuseness:

Even years ago I revealed a great deal to you. But now let me take off in complete freedom. Do not restrain me in my flight in the name of what I said a decade past during this or that lesson. . . .

Did I not share everything with all of you then, as I do today? Do you really think that I ever kept secret the best of my knowledge? But I cannot help it if, having never stopped working, I have learned a great deal, especially about this divine freedom that is to music the air without which it would die. What would you say of a scientist or of a painter who, like stagnant water, would stop his experimentation and remain still? . . .

'You will wreak havoc'! you exclaimed.

Do I have to take into consideration non-musical, clumsy people, but, worst of all, pedants who – and this is serious – number my thoughts, label and file them, although they understand nothing of their spirit. . . ?

Was music created for musicologists? Did Bach write for teachers' meetings?

The most beautiful thing in the world is precisely the conjunction of learning and inspiration. Oh the passion for research and the joy of discovery!

I followed my vocation and never ceased to work without ever compromising. That is all. . . .[12]

The proliferation of early music in recent years has to a great extent been connected with a reaction against nineteenth-century musical traditions. One very fine harpsichordist, when asked a few years ago how he felt about the music of Beethoven, Brahms and other nineteenth-century composers, replied after considerable hesitation, 'I respect them.' This sort of snobbishness about the superiority of early music to what came after it is just as absurd as the opposite attitude; and since Landowska's name is forever linked with the early music revival, it would be easy to think of her as one of the perpetrators of this silliness. Nothing could be further from the truth. Raised on a musical diet of Chopin and other standard repertoire composers, she never came to regard their music with anything other than love and admiration. She simply wished to enrich the concert literature by incorporating into it those great treasures of the past which had fallen into oblivion. Today, she is occasionally laughed at by people who do not realize that her very individualistic style was not only a result of her strong personality and nineteenth-century upbringing: it must also be remembered that all her life she was forced to demonstrate to the unconverted that the harpsichord was not, after all, a 'soulless' instrument.

It has been said that a strong society is one which is not afraid to destroy its past. We in the last quarter of the twentieth century have quite understandably become obsessed with the past, for ours is a society so weak that it cannot refrain from destroying its future. We feel happier, more protected, in museums, in our history, than in the present, perhaps because history, regarded superficially, provides the comforting illusion that the continuity of human effort is to be taken for granted. Today there are relatively few who want to hear the serious works of their contemporaries: good or bad, those works are too distressingly accurate a reflection of our time. It appears that we can only drag ourselves forward by staring backward over our shoulders, for the future is too horrifying to contemplate.

Even without Landowska, the twentieth century would have rediscovered the music of the past. We were ripe for that consolation. But she brought it to us with conviction, zeal and charm – rare qualities in any age.

Chapter Eight

Vladimir Horowitz

❖❖❖❖❖❖❖❖❖❖❖❖❖❖❖❖❖❖❖❖❖❖❖❖❖❖❖❖❖❖❖❖❖❖

I have observed that in the so-called virtuoso concert, audiences every-where in the world behave in the same way. I noticed, as a listener to such 'virtuoso' concerts, that people are always happier at nine o'clock than they are at eight o'clock, with no exception. I call the first hour of such programmes the 'duty part' and the second hour the 'family part'. During the first hour people hardly listen, are rather indifferent, uninterested. Only when it comes nearer to the encores, do they warm up. Yet the better pieces of music have, for the most part, been played in the first hour.

Artur Schnabel, *My Life and Music*.[1]

A RETIRED LONDON concert agent who represented many of the most important musicians of this century was recently asked to name the pianist who, during the past fifty years, has had a greater influence than any other on his younger colleagues. He named two: Artur Schnabel and Vladimir Horowitz. Schnabel, he said, was a deep and subtle musician who had changed many pianists' approach to programming by proving that not all audiences have to be stuffed with empty showpieces; while Horowitz had so jolted other pianists through the brilliance and daring of his playing that none of them was able to remain unaffected.

The juxtaposition of Schnabel and Horowitz is an odd but interesting one; for Schnabel, like Anton Rubinstein, saw his task as both musical and instructive, while Horowitz was and is an atavistic phenomenon whose point of view as a performer is closer to those of Paganini and Liszt than to those of his nearer ancestors. People normally went to Schnabel recitals in order to hear intelligent performances of Mozart or Beethoven or Schubert. They go to Horowitz recitals in order to hear Horowitz. This does not mean that Horowitz's performances are necessarily unintelligent; but initially, at least, one listens to Horowitz in the same way that one looks up at a shooting star: it is obviously dazzling; and it is difficult not to be awed by that aspect of it.

Horowitz has now been before the public for over sixty years, off and on, and his grip on audiences seems as firm as ever. He is also as disputed a figure as ever. So often one hears this or that pianist described as 'a good, solid technician and musician, perhaps not very exciting, but always reliable'. No one would dream of characterizing Horowitz in that way. His technique is brilliant, his musicianship questionable, his performances always exciting but often maddening. There are times when it seems as if he is capable only of beguiling or shocking his public, loving or bludgeoning it, but not of confronting it calmly. This is not always the case; but it happens often enough to make one wonder whether this strange man is the great artist that his admirers claim he is, or simply the beneficiary – and perhaps also the victim – of an extraordinary central nervous system and an equally great sensitivity to tone colour.

Horowitz came from a very musical and well-to-do Russian Jewish family. His father, an electrical engineer who represented both Westinghouse and the German Allgemeine Elektrische Gesellschaft in Kiev, played the cello; and his mother was a fine amateur pianist. An elder brother taught violin at the Moscow Conservatory and a younger sister established herself in Russia as a concert pianist in her own right. Even the Kiev street on which Horowitz was born on 1 October 1904 was called Musikalnyi Pereulok – Musical Lane. His mother gave him his earliest piano instruction when he was six; by the time he was nine his exceptional talent had shown itself and he was sent to the Kiev Conservatory. When he was fifteen he began studying, still at the Kiev Conservatory, with Felix Blumenfeld, who had been a pupil of Rubinstein. The young Horowitz's main interest was in composition; but by the time he reached Leningrad the Revolution had impoverished his family. Although still a student, he began to play in public. At the age of eighteen, a year after his graduation from the Conservatory, he gave a highly successful series of concerts in Kharkov that marked the real beginning of his career. Soon he began touring Russia; and in those troubled times he was often paid in foodstuffs rather than cash.

At his Berlin début in 1926, Horowitz was received with great enthusiasm, and what was to have been a temporary absence from his native country became a permanent one. Everywhere he went he aroused tremendous excitement, and his American début (1928) in the Tchaikovsky First Piano Concerto with the

New York Philharmonic under Sir Thomas Beecham was a particularly important moment in his career. (He eventually became an American citizen.) In 1933 he married Wanda Toscanini, the youngest of the conductor's children; and the following year the Horowitzes' only child, a daughter, was born.

The first of his extended withdrawals from the concert platform took place between 1936 and 1939. Rumours that he had undergone a serious operation, that he had had a nervous breakdown and that he was receiving treatment for other medical problems all circulated widely; but Horowitz has never publicly cleared the matter up. He reappeared at the Lucerne Festival in 1939 playing Brahms' Second Piano Concerto under Toscanini's direction, and under great strain.

Although Horowitz resumed his career and continued to play many concerts during the next fourteen years, he remained as nervous, hypochondriacal and unwilling a performer as he had always been, and often cancelled appearances for any number of reasons. (The American pianist and raconteur Oscar Levant, himself a notorious hypochondriac, once proposed forming a duo-piano team with Horowitz so that they could cancel concerts together.) In 1953 Horowitz again stopped playing. Again there were rumours of a breakdown; and this time his retirement lasted twelve years. In an interview published many years later, Horowitz said:

When I used to tour, I took the train. I didn't sleep well, I didn't eat well. I didn't even like the train. Four concerts a week and travelling on the train were just too much. I suddenly felt very tired and decided to take a year off. Then, you see, I enjoyed the peaceful life so much, I kept on taking year after year off. [2]

When asked whether he had been institutionalized, he replied: 'I guess human nature is prone to respond more to bad news rather than good news. Anyhow, in those twelve years I made seven recordings, so I guess I couldn't have been mad if I did that.' [3] All of which is neither a yes nor a no.

When it was announced in 1965 that Horowitz would be returning to Carnegie Hall for a recital, such excitement was generated in the press and among the public that the pianist's wife told *The New York Times*, 'Horowitz is like a fifth Beatle.' Ticket prices were raised and thousands of people could not be accommodated. Clearly Horowitz was satisfied with the critical and financial results of the experiment, for he gave more

167

concerts, albeit sporadically and on his own terms (afternoon recitals only, no long-distance travel from New York and extremely high fees). There was another withdrawal accompanied by more rumours in the early 1970s, and another less publicized comeback a few years later, at about the time of the death of his daughter, Sonia. Late in 1981 he was still playing with exceptional success and was even contemplating his first European appearances in several decades.

During most of his career, Horowitz's repertoire has centred on Romantic and post-Romantic composers like Chopin, Schumann, Rachmaninov and Scriabin. Of course he has played a great deal of other music, too; but these composers seem to interest him most. He has claimed that his reason for concentrating on a brilliant repertoire is the size of his audiences. 'Today [1950] my smallest audience is in Carnegie Hall [capacity approximately three thousand]; more usually I play to five or six thousand people. I must program music that will be communicated. . . . If you play classic music in correct style on a big piano and in a big hall, it will bore most of the audience. This is not the listeners' shortcoming. It just demonstrates that classic music was written for small pianos and small rooms.'[4]

This of course implies that those who are interested in the music of Bach, Mozart, Beethoven and others would enjoy hearing Horowitz play that music; and that is by no means to be assumed. On the contrary, it is both difficult and unpleasant to imagine a Horowitz confrontation with *The Well-Tempered Clavier* or the slow movement of the *'Hammerklavier'* Sonata. Nearly thirty years ago B. H. Haggin wrote devastatingly in this regard:

. . . the alternation of brio and affettuoso teasing that is the sum total of Horowitz's playing would make Mozart, Beethoven and Schubert intolerable even to a few hundred of the thousands who, long before the Horowitz era, used to listen to Josef Hofmann play one of the last Beethoven sonatas, and in recent years filled Hunter College Auditorium to hear Schnabel play these works and sonatas of Mozart and Schubert. And on the other hand Schnabel's performances of these works would bore even a few hundred of the thousands who attend Horowitz recitals to be alternately excited by his supercharged virtuosity and titillated by his affettuoso teasing. The true Horowitz situation is that of a pianist and an audience on the same level of understanding. . . .[5]

Haggin also refers to Horowitz's 'fussing with tone and phrase-contour with no regard for the character and requirements of the music'.[6] But what, then, of the music that Horowitz does play regularly? Let us take as an example his recording (dating from the 1960s) of Schumann's *Fantasy*. The first movement, as he plays it, lacks breadth: it is harsh rather than big. The eighteen bars which open this piece constitute a single, extended statement; and if ever a statement demanded to be declared as a unit, it is this one. Horowitz plays it crudely, in small jerks. A little further on, in the section marked *Im Legenden-Ton*, Schumann has written a number of *ritardandi* and *a tempi*; but Horowitz goes too far, pushing and pulling the music completely out of shape. His staccato playing, later in the same section, is desiccated. At the return to the opening theme, he plays the right hand's first three octaves very loudly, then drops – unexpectedly, illogically and contrary to Schumann's instructions – to a piano. On the last page, his *ritardandi* begin too soon and are exaggerated, and the last fourteen bars are almost embarrassingly mawkish. Neither his carefully contrived *rubati* nor his carefully balanced chords make much sense in the context. The second movement begins excellently – firmly but not aggressively; but the first quiet section (bars twenty-two *et seq.*) is played with such excessive delicacy that the forward-moving tension of the piece is immediately lost. From that point on Horowitz continues to divide the movement into massive, thumping sections and chirpy, trivial ones. In the *Etwas langsamer* middle part he never achieves real lightness because he cannot resist banging out (as opposed to bringing out) the melody; and this annoying accentuation becomes positively oppressive as he approaches the retransition to the main theme. He also exaggerates the passing of the melody from one voice to another (eighteen bars *et seq.* before the coda). And nothing could be less spontaneous, less exciting, more unmusical than his handling of the coda itself. The third movement is equally eccentric, though not as irritatingly so. The modulatory cadences fall flat and the coda clangs and jangles. All in all, the playing is so inflated that it gets in the way of the music.

Horowitz's recording, made many years earlier, of Chopin's B minor Scherzo is another study in self-indulgence. His opening tempo is terrifyingly fast, and justifiably so; but his dry-as-dust, cast-off phrase endings are not justifiable, nor is the gruff, military style of the *agitato* section (bars sixty-nine *et seq.*), nor the exaggerated wallop sustained by the bass notes at bars 117 to 124. Horowitz begins the lyrical middle section, which Chopin has marked *sotto voce e ben legato* (whispered and very smooth) by over-emphasizing the melody in the alto voice. He destroys the lovely simplicity of this music by applying fresh makeup to it every four bars. Bars 548 to 569, immediately preceding the coda, are played perfunctorily, with little change in dynamics; and the concluding passage itself, despite a forceful beginning, brilliant arpeggios and chromatic scales and some gimmicky rumbling (bars 589 to 592), also seems almost nonchalant, anticlimactic.

There is no reason to be surprised by any of this: Horowitz himself has stated his attitude to interpretation. He has said that a performer 'may sit down and play one passage one way and then perhaps exaggerate the next, but, in any event, he must do something with the music. The worst thing is not to do anything. It may even be something you don't like, but do it!'[7] In other words, not only is it acceptable, according to Horowitz, for a musician to choose not to try to understand a composer's intentions: it is also perfectly reasonable that he not have any overall vision at all of the work. He may simply play this bit or that according to his mood of the moment.

Yet Horowitz can provide some pleasant musical experiences in unexpected areas. I was surprised to hear the great Haydn expert H. C. Robbins Landon state that although it is all to the good that more musicians are starting to play pre-nineteenth-century works on replicas of the instruments for which they were intended, in his opinion no one has yet equalled Horowitz's performance on a modern grand piano of Haydn's last sonata, in E-flat major (Hob. XVI/52). Haydn is not a composer with whom Horowitz's name is generally associated; but a thirty-year-old Horowitz recording of this work bears out Landon's opinion. The first movement is beautiful, even if one may legitimately quibble with Horowitz's pedalling. In the second movement Horowitz's phrases are long and lyrical, and Haydn's intricate rhythms are finely controlled. (The octaves, bars 28 to 32, are, admittedly, a bit Tchaikovskian.) Best of all is the last movement played with brilliance and a sense of fun. There is no pounding of the forte chords; and in fact an extraordinary lightness is maintained throughout. Similarly, Horowitz's recording of Beethoven's 'Waldstein' Sonata (C major, Op. 53) is remarkable for its restraint. Although I find this 'Waldstein' performance much too dry and miniaturized, I admire Horowitz's clear sense of the form of the work and the good judgment he shows in refusing to toy with each phrase and section.

Other recordings in which Horowitz manages to keep his perverse streak in check include several concerti conducted by Toscanini, Fritz Reiner and others; and the best among those I have heard include the two versions (1941 and 1943) of Tchaikovsky's First Piano Concerto, both under Toscanini's direction, and the 1951 version of Rachmaninov's Third Piano Concerto with Reiner. Horowitz has called his friendship with Rachmaninov 'one of the greatest inspirations in my life',[8] and it is well known that Rachmaninov was a great admirer of his young compatriot's playing. (Rachmaninov's opinion counts a great deal: he was an outstanding pianist himself, and he had heard nearly every important keyboard artist from Anton Rubinstein onwards.) In each movement of this recording, it is difficult to decide what to admire most in Horowitz's playing: his shading of tone is marvellous, the variety in his phrasing remarkable and the brilliance of the virtuosic passages nearly incredible. His performance of the last movement gives us a clue as to why serious musicians and critics of a century-and-a-half ago dropped all attempts at concrete analysis of Paganini's playing and resorted to words like 'demonic' and 'diabolic'. There is a combination of white heat and terrible coldness in Horowitz's playing that transforms a musical experience into a physical one.

More important than what Horowitz himself refers to as his 'so-called phenomenal technique' is his audacity. His playing, even on record, is not always absolutely clean and note-perfect; but where he seems to form a class of his own is in his ability to fling himself at the keyboard, to dare himself to play with a Dionysian madness so intense that it makes our brains reel. He says that 'the pianist should never be afraid to take risks. When I play for audiences, I take risks. Sometimes they're correct, sometimes they are not. But I am not afraid to take risks. . . .'[9] But while Paganini in his day took risks almost entirely with his own music, Horowitz takes them with the music of others; and if it is true that some of his most satisfying recordings from a musical as opposed to a purely pianistic point of view are of concerti and pre-Romantic repertoire, one is strongly tempted to conclude that he functions best when the fear of God has been put into him by strict classical forms or when he has to contend with other performers whose artistic personalities may be even stronger than his own.

Some would disagree with this opinion. American pianist John Browning concurred with a friend's observation that Horowitz 'could take a very structured piece like a Beethoven sonata or a Chopin nocturne and distort it, and yet could take a very floundering form like a Scriabin sonata and play it tight as a drum.'[10] The fact is that Horowitz's playing is so unpredictable that nearly all generalizations about it are sometimes right and sometimes wrong.

When I said earlier that Schnabel's public seemed, on the whole, to be primarily interested in *what* he played, while Horowitz's seems more interested in *how* he plays, I did not mean to turn this distinction into a moral judgment. Even those who believe it is sinful to enjoy Horowitz's recording of *Stars and Stripes Forever* or his *Carmen Fantasy* will have to admit that the sin is a fairly harmless one, in view of the general condition of the world as a whole. Nevertheless, I believe that it is dangerous to regard Horowitz's or anyone else'e technique as an art in itself; and I also believe that most musicians find Horowitz's way with the standard repertoire cloying, although they may be amazed by his playing in general and enlightened by certain of its details. His eccentricities may fascinate, but in the end, they remain eccentricities. As Bernard Shaw said, 'the "classical" players have the best of it in the long run.'

Horowitz and the mechanics of his playing have undeniably interested other pianists for over half a century. Schnabel first heard him in Leningrad in 1923 and was 'very impressed'.

He even wanted a lesson with me, but I decided he was not in need of any. I also asked him whether he was composing and he said, very shyly, 'Yes'. He had an enormous success, was rather spoiled, and tired. He gave twenty recitals a season in one city. He was really the hero at that time. I thought it was absolutely necessary for him physically and mentally to leave Russia. I am very glad he followed my advice.[11]

Even the aging Paderewski heard Horowitz in Chicago around 1930 and commented:

I must admit that I liked him very much; I liked both his playing and his general bearing. . . . He was self-disciplined, and, above all, he has rhythm and tone. I only heard him play the D Minor Concerto by Rachmaninoff, but it was very fine indeed. Of course I cannot tell how he tackles the great classical composers, what he does with Bach,

Beethoven, Chopin or Schumann. If he does not get spoiled, and if he can keep up his present power, he ought to go very far. . . . Without any doubt he is the most convincing among the younger pianists.[12]

Artur Rubinstein was very upset by Horowitz's successes. In the second and more fatuous part of his autobiography he comments acridly on his relations with Horowitz; and although some of what he says is probably true, it is sad that at the age of ninety – and at the close of an overwhelmingly successful career – Rubinstein should still have been rehashing old grudges over recording contracts of forty years earlier and the like.

Many pianists of the generation after Horowitz's have remained fascinated by his technique and his sound. John Browning, in criticizing young pianists today, said that 'they have to be made to understand the importance of thinking in orchestral terms at the keyboard. . . . All they bring to the piano is fingers. They haven't had their imaginations awakened to sound like Horowitz, for example, who can play ten voices and make them sound like ten different instruments. They just don't grasp that element of sound.'[13] And elsewhere Browning says that 'even if he does something that might set my teeth on edge, I just ignore it because I'm positive that there will be something in the performance that will completely dazzle me.'[14]

Even as subtle a musician as Vladimir Ashkenazy finds some aspects of Horowitz's playing irresistible; and in criticizing the notion of a clearly identifiable 'Russian school' of piano technique he commented: 'I've heard it said that Horowitz, for example, plays with an outstretched hand, almost flat-fingered, and that that is characteristic of the Russian school. . . . I, too, think that Horowitz plays with flat fingers.' And he adds, 'I've never seen anyone else in Russia or any place else play like him.'[15]

Some of the half-dozen young men whom Horowitz has accepted as pupils at various times have also remarked on his playing.* Ivan Davis reported:

One time, when we were playing octaves, Horowitz said to me, 'You know, you've got a good wrist, most people don't have good wrists. Want me to show you how I play my octaves?' And I thought, 'Here it is,

---

*These remarks appeared in an article entitled 'The Secret Career of Horowitz' by Glenn Plaskin, in *The New York Times Magazine*, 11 May 1980. Mr Plaskin is preparing a complete biography of Horowitz.

the secret that all the world's been waiting for.' Horowitz said, 'I practice slow, high from the wrist and in different rhythms.' Of course, *everybody* practices that way, so I didn't learn one thing!

Once Horowitz told me that he thought his playing had the best of the masculine and feminine qualities. He said that some men are incapable of feminine warmth while a lot of feminine players did not have the aggressive masculine quality. . . . I've also been told that he jokingly said there were three kinds of pianists: Jewish pianists, homosexual pianists and bad pianists!

To Gary Graffman, Horowitz spoke about projection:

Horowitz told me that some things that may have sounded beautiful in his living room would have been lost in a large hall. He prepared me for pitfalls I might encounter rehearsing with orchestras, showed me how to practice problem passages – for instance, octaves in the Tchaikovsky Concerto – but he was most concerned with communicating across the footlights. Horowitz, always cognizant of his audience, wanted a big sound that would embrace and intoxicate his listeners.

Some of the students noticed his personal oddities. Alexander Fiorillo once went to see Horowitz when the latter was ill.

His bedroom looked like an apothecary's shop. I never saw so much medication. Bottles everywhere. Black drapes and black shades drawn in the middle of an afternoon in July! Horowitz was lying on his back with his eyes covered with plastic eye shades and he was wearing ear plugs. He always complained to me about his stomach problems.

(Someone who once commented innocently to Sonia Horowitz that it must be wonderful to have genius on both sides of one's family received the wry response: 'Yes, from my father I inherited a tendency toward spastic colitis, and from my grandfather [Toscanini], dandruff.') Partly as a result of his nervous stomach, Horowitz has gone through several food fads, one of which was observed by Fiorillo:

He would eat nothing but lamb patties and would invite me to join him. They were the most tasteless food imaginable and he ate them for lunch and dinner every day. Before bedtime, for variety, he would have Ry-Krisp and milk or tea.

One friend of the Toscanini family told me that at the conductor's funeral in New York in 1957, Horowitz arrived at the last moment and made it known that he could not proceed without his tea and crackers; so Toscanini's son, Walter, had to run out and get Horowitz what he required before the funeral could begin. Many artists believe that their whims should be the major preoccupation of all who come in contact with them; but if even a small portion of the stories told about Horowitz is true, he is a particularly difficult case.

Davis tells of accompanying Horowitz to a Carnegie Hall concert given by Rudolf and Peter Serkin.

After the concert, in the midst of the backstage autograph seekers, Horowitz kept looking at his watch. I thought he was panic-stricken with all the people surrounding him. But this was not the problem. We got into the car and he said, 'Got to get home because the Emmy Awards are on television and I've got to see if "Naked City" wins.' This was his favourite show.

It is said that Horowitz is today the highest-paid instrumentalist in the classical music field, and that he earns as much as $40,000 for a single performance. Statistics of this sort are always more interesting for what they tell us about audience psychology than as indications of the artistic value of the performer. A Horowitz recital provides excitement. However much one may disagree with his ideas, with his self-confessed wilfulness in confronting the music he plays, one must admit that he challenges himself musically and technically – that he is not content to rely upon past achievements. For that reason, the gladiatorial aspect of concert giving, which one does not feel at all with some artists, is especially pronounced in Horowitz's case. The question of whether or not he will be able to succeed in playing a certain section at a certain speed takes precedence over the question of whether or not that tempo makes sense in terms of the tempi he has chosen for other sections. His daring, his bravura, instead of remaining simply a means, become the primary object of attention. This provides tremendous amusement when he is playing an arrangement of a Paganini *Caprice*, for example; but the fun palls considerably when the Horowitz method is applied to Schumann or Chopin.

Horowitz has often been called a twentieth-century Liszt; and one recalls Amy Fay's perceptive comment regarding the effect that Liszt's playing made upon listeners: 'You feel at once that . . . *you* are nothing but his puppet, and somehow you take a base delight in the humiliation!'

Chapter Nine

Glenn Gould

❖❖❖❖❖❖❖❖❖❖❖❖❖❖❖❖❖❖❖❖❖❖❖❖❖❖❖❖❖❖❖❖❖❖❖❖

GLENN GOULD is not only the last of this book's subjects: he is also
the most difficult one to write about. His career as an international concert artist lasted, by his own choice, only nine
years; the recordings he has made during the intervening time
have been controversial; his personal and professional eccentricities have often attracted more attention than his qualities as
a musician; and his numerous writings and pronouncements on
a wide range of subjects have not always clarified our understanding of his aims and achievements.

Gould is also, in several senses, a misfit in this book. He has
neither attained nor attempted to attain the heights of international celebrity reached by the protagonists of the previous
chapters, and his renunciation of traditional concert life makes it
nearly impossible that he will do so in the future. The personal
magnetism that characterized all of them and the flamboyance of
some of them are totally foreign to him. Yet the originality and
fundamental musical talent of this pianist bear comparison with
any of his predecessors or contemporaries.

The real reason for including him in this study, however, is
that he represents, or seems to represent, a new development in
the history of his profession. Since 1964, when he last played in
public, his reputation has been based entirely on the recordings
which he has continued to make on a regular basis. I say 'seems
to represent' because from Caruso's day onward, most performing musicians have in fact used the gramophone for the dual
purpose of broadening their fame and earning power while they
are alive and establishing a reputation that will outlive them.
The difference is that for most of them, recordings have been or
are an adjunct to their careers, while for Gould, the performing
years were a necessary evil that made his name known sufficiently to enable him to rely exclusively on recordings
thereafter.

29. Kiev-born Vladimir Horowitz (b. 1904) began to make an enormous impact in western Europe and America during the late 1920s. His superb keyboard control and questionable musicianship made him a controversial performer from the very outset of his career.

30, 31. Several times Horowitz has withdrawn from active concert life for extended periods, but he has always returned to resume a high position among pianists and in the public estimate. Here Horowitz plays at Carnegie Hall in 1965 following a twelve-year absence from the concert platform.

A more recent photograph of the pianist acknowledging applause at
a performance.

32, 33. (*Opposite*) Horowitz has been an avid art collector for many years. Here he is seen in front of a painting by Georges Rouault which he owned at one time. (*Above*) A portrait photograph of the pianist later in life.

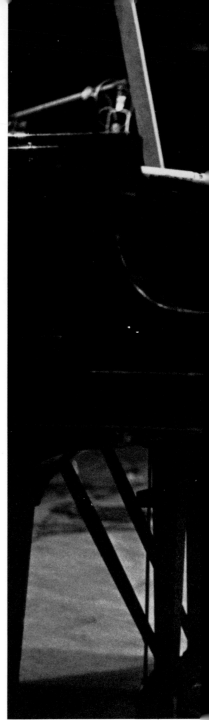

34, 35. Canadian pianist Glenn Gould was born in 1932 – almost exactly 150 years after the birth of Paganini – but he appears to represent the antithesis of what is generally believed to be the virtuoso mentality. His career as an international concert artist lasted, by his own choice, only nine years, and since 1964 he has based his musical reputation upon his controversial recordings. (*Above*) Gould during his touring period, *c.* 1960. Note the characteristically low elbows and flattened hand position. (*Opposite*) Gould in the recording studio. He sits lower in relation to the piano than any other pianist of note. His battered chair is low in itself, and the piano's legs are raised on wooden blocks.

36. Gould in casual mood.

When my friends and I, in our early teens, were first beginning to attend concerts enthusiastically in the years around 1960, there were two pianists whom we looked forward to hearing as often as possible. The first was Artur Rubinstein, the grand old man, who sat ramrod-straight at the piano, who adored being adored by his audience, whose concerts always seemed to be gala events and who made us feel that we were in direct communication with a bygone age. The second was Gould, who lurched onto the stage looking as if he had rolled out of bed half-a-minute earlier, stared dazedly at the audience, sang and grunted loudly as he played, crossed his legs under and bent his head over the keyboard, occasionally flailed the air with a free arm, and bowed clumsily while attempting to keep his shirttails from coming out of his trousers. He also plunged us into the structural hearts of Bach, Beethoven and others in new and startling ways, exposing his vision of the music by means of a technique that was at once terrifyingly secure and free of any exhibitionism. We in Cleveland were told that George Szell had said of Gould, 'That nut is a genius'; and if we came at first to see the nut, we returned to hear the genius. I particularly remember performances of the Bach D minor and Beethoven C minor concerti in 1962 – one of those concerts at which a music student feels he has lived through several years of instruction in a few minutes. H. H. Stuckenschmidt, the German music historian, called Gould the greatest pianist he had heard since Busoni, and Heinrich Neuhaus, the legendary Soviet pedagogue, wrote that Gould's way of playing Bach made one feel that the composer himself was sitting at the keyboard. We youngsters were certainly convinced then that Gould would inevitably come to be considered the most outstanding pianist of our time.

Born in Toronto on 25 September 1932, Gould is easily the best-known instrumentalist Canada has yet produced.* His parents were both greatly interested in music, and his mother was his only teacher from the time he began to play the piano at the age of three until he was ten. He did not get on well with other children, disliked school intensely and left high school

---

*Strangely enough, Canada, like Australia, has been somewhat under-average in turning out internationally famous instrumentalists but very prolific in its outstanding singers. Canadian singers born between the two world wars, like Gould, include sopranos Lois Marshall and Teresa Stratas, contralto Maureen Forrester, tenors Jon Vickers and Léopold Simoneau and bass-baritone George London.

without receiving a diploma. His piano studies with Alberto Guerrero at Toronto's Royal Conservatory began when he was ten and lasted until he was nearly twenty; and he also studied the organ and theory at the same institution.

Gould gave many recitals during his teens. His unusual talent was quickly recognized, and by the time he was twenty he had been heard numerous times on the Canadian Broadcasting Corporation's radio network and in concert with most of the best Canadian orchestras. But his international career was launched early in 1955 when he gave début recitals in Washington and New York. The programme for these two performances was an extraordinary one: it included pieces by Orlando Gibbons and Jan Sweelinck, five three-part Inventions and the G major Partita by Bach, Beethoven's Sonata Op. 109, Webern's Variations Op. 27 and the Berg Sonata. The reviews were outstanding, and within twenty-four hours of the New York recital the twenty-two-year-old pianist had signed an exclusive contract with Columbia (CBS) Records – the first such contract that that company had ever undertaken with an unfledged artist. Five months later Gould returned to New York to make his first Columbia recording, Bach's 'Goldberg' Variations; and it was the amazing success of that record which brought him world-wide attention.

Concert and recital engagements came in great abundance. Gould played throughout the United States, Canada, western Europe, Israel and the USSR (the first Canadian musician and first North American pianist to perform in Russia). His discography grew steadily, he appeared on radio and television, his String Quartet was performed and published, he lectured at universities and elsewhere, the National Film Board of Canada produced a short film about him and his name appeared frequently in magazines and newspapers, both as the author of articles on a variety of topics and as the subject of interviews and other studies. It was known that he kept bottled water next to the piano while he played, refused to shake hands with anyone, carried a dilapidated and very low piano stool with him from town to town on his tours, believed that concerti (in which solo instrument and orchestra alternate in carrying the principal part) are immorally competitive, hummed and sang a counterpoint to what he was playing; and all these peculiarities attracted newspaper feature writers and brought Gould added notoriety.

In Chicago's Orchestra Hall on 28 March 1964 he gave a recital which consisted of Bach's Partita in D major and excerpts from *The Art of the Fugue*, Beethoven's Sonata Op. 110 and Ernst Křenek's Sonata No. 3. Gould was then thirty-one years old; he has not performed in public since that date. What he has done during the years away from the footlights, apart from making a substantial number of recordings, of which more later, has been to bring forth a river of words; for Gould is both highly analytical and highly articulate – even loquacious. It is almost as if he has been trying to compensate for his niggardliness as a performer and for his partial disappearance from the public eye by flooding us with his opinions on a great variety of subjects, musical and otherwise. It has been possible for the public to follow his ideas on morality and piano regulation, life in northern Canada and ecstasy, Pablo Casals and Petula Clark, Bach played on the Moog synthesizer (he likes it) and Leopold Stokowski, Muzak (he approves of it) and Schoenberg, and much, much more. In Canada he is something of a sacred cow – one who, according to many people, is allowed to rampage through the CBC's sound effects department rather too often. To discuss the thoughts he has expressed is to plunge oneself into a morass; yet he has made it virtually impossible to examine his work as a musician without also examining at least some of his ideas.

Gould is a man in love with technology because, as he says, it enables him 'to exist as far as possible from the outside world and have contact with it electronically.'[1] It would probably be inaccurate to say that he is afraid of that outside world; but his writings and published comments give the impression that he is repelled by it, by other people, and certainly by physical contact with other people. Clearly, he thinks of concert audiences as a sort of 'herd' phenomenon, but not, as one might suspect, because the majority of those in attendance are unlikely to understand his musical intentions and accomplishments. To him, an audience is a group of 'people sitting there with the perspiration of two thousand, nine hundred and ninety-nine others penetrating their nostrils.'[2] His keep-cool-and-don't-touch-me attitude leads him to some astonishing conclusions on extra-musical subjects, too:

A war, for instance, engaged in by computer-aimed missiles, is a slightly better, less objectionable war, than one fought by clubs or spears. Not *much* better, and unquestionably more destructive, statistically, but better to the extent, at least, that, all things being equal, the adrenal response of the participants . . . is less engaged by it. . . .[3]

By this nonsensical reasoning, a general who calmly orders a group of soldiers to destroy a town and its inhabitants is a 'slightly better' man than the subordinates who then do the physical damage.

Statements like these are just the thing to ignite the imaginations of all self-respecting amateur psychologists. And although a book about music is not the place for such speculations, his remarks have been cited because they illustrate the complicated philosophy he has created in order to explain his distaste for public performance and for direct human contact in general. That he prefers the grey North to the sunny South, sleeping by day to sleeping by night and maintaining his relationships with others by telephone rather than in person tells us more than a lot of high-falutin' technological pseudo-philosophy can possibly do about his withdrawal from the world. At the time when he renounced the concert circuit he was quoted as having said: 'As I grow older I find more and more that I can do without [people]; I separate myself from conflicting and contrasting notions. Monastic seclusion works for me.'[4] That, of course, is his right. And it is only human, given this attitude, that he should consequently consider solitude to be 'the condition of heroism. One can't feel oneself heroic without having first been cast off by the world, or perhaps by having done the casting-off oneself. . . .'[5]

In many ways, it is easy to sympathize with him. To a man of his temperament, 'the stage' was not a source of joy:

I used to take my pulse rate just before a concert out of scientific curiosity, and it was always very fast. So there was obviously a kind of unnatural excitement. But it wasn't the sort that paralyzed me with fear, if only because I had a kind of indifference to the whole process. I was really counting off the years and the number of events within those years that would be necessary to make it possible for me to forget the whole thing. I think if I had really been dependent upon it, or known that I had to be for a very long time, it would have depressed me so horribly that I would have been just miserable. I was, up to a point, miserable anyway. . . .[6]

Like Horowitz, Gould was and may still be nervous and hypo-chondriacal. He frequently cancelled performances and, when he did perform, depended upon tranquillizers and sedatives to keep him going. It is no surprise, then, that once he had earned a substantial sum of money and established an international repu-

188

tation, he elected to stop giving concerts and to devote a great part of his energies to recording. He admits that he could not have organized his life according to his ideals had he not first submitted to nearly a decade of concert-giving.

Gould reasons that recordings permit the performer and producer to select the acoustic environment they find desirable, to achieve a degree of clarity not possible in the concert hall, to delve into areas of repertoire which might not attract a wide enough audience to warrant public concerts, and to improve a performance by splicing together material from two or more 'takes'. This is all fairly straightforward. But he goes off the deep end when he claims that modern recording technology has created 'a new kind of listener – a listener more participant in the musical experience.'[7] He exalts advanced forms of dial-twiddling to the status of creativity:

Let us say, for example, that you enjoy Bruno Walter's performance of the exposition and recapitulation from the first movement of Beethoven's Fifth Symphony but incline toward Klemperer's handling of the development section, which employs a notably divergent tempo. . . . With the pitch-speed correlation held in abeyance, you could snip out these measures from the Klemperer edition and splice them into the Walter performance without having the splice produce either an alteration of tempo or a fluctuation of pitch. . . .[8]

For Gould, this represents one possible means of returning to what he sees as a pre-Baroque-period attitude towards music: the composer, performer and listener are united in the same individual. This is absurd, in the first place because although there was generally little distinction between composer and performer in those days, most listeners were incapable of either composing or performing, just as is the case today; and it is absurd in the second place because the senseless activity of patching together two or more versions of a work can in no way be compared to the achievement of composing or playing even the most elementary piece. If I, as a person who loves the art of painting but cannot manipulate a brush myself, were to remove the head of Christ from one print of Piero della Francesca's 'Resurrection' and stick it on the body of a different print of the same painting, I would not expect to be credited with creative powers for having done so – even if I had made sure that the proportions were correct.

There is a great deal of truth in what Gould says about the

189

preferability of recordings to live concerts. I do not feel physically contaminated by the people sitting around me, as appears to be the case with Gould, nor do I agree with his contention that many members of the public 'want blood' – want the artist to have a memory lapse or to be humiliated in some other way; but I do heartily agree that the absurd nineteenth-century formal attire which most artists still feel compelled to don, the rituals of applause and acknowledgment, the often unacceptable sound quality in certain areas of most halls and the sometimes grotesque inattentiveness of a substantial segment of the public are all factors which work against the music itself. I think that those of us who have grown up listening seriously to recordings (as opposed to letting them run while dealing with other activities) find that our concentration is generally much better at home than in a public auditorium. One may listen to what one pleases when one pleases and in performances by musicians, dead or alive, whom one trusts. And as someone who – unlike Gould – is categorically opposed to background music, I appreciate being able to interrupt my listening if I find that my concentration is wandering.

Yet the concert as an institution must be defended. For young musicians, it is useful, desirable and in most cases necessary to see as well as to hear already-established artists. One learns about technique almost as much through the eyes as through the ears; and although a truly extraordinary aural ability may be able to compensate for lack of visual assistance, I see no reason for denying anyone this form of instruction. It also remains as true today as in the past that there is no better way of encouraging musically gifted children to work harder at their studies than to take them to concerts. The whole concert atmosphere is usually intoxicating to such children, and biographies of performing musicians are filled with stories of 'the night I heard Kreisler (or Casals or Rubinstein) and decided that someday I, too, would be a musician'. A typical story is one recounted by a famous pianist who, at the age of six, was taken to hear Josef Hofmann, and on whom the concert made

a staggering impression. . . . When I was being brought home in the car, I was in that wonderful state of half-awakeness in which you hear all sorts of incredible sounds going through your mind. They were all *orchestral* sounds, but *I* was playing them all, and suddenly I was Hofmann. I was enchanted.[9]

Is it necessary to add that this particular young listener was Glenn Gould?

Gould distrusts things Latin – bullfights and Italian opera, for instance. But what of those of us decadent enough to like opera? It seems unarguable that many outstanding musicians, from Monteverdi to Mozart to Verdi and on down to our own day, have produced great music for the theatre; and although some opera recordings are wonderful, they cannot take the place of the real thing. For the most part, great operas were written by great men of the theatre who intended their music to be one among several essential components. Opera on film has so far proved to be rather dismal from an artistic point of view; and although I am entirely in favour of video cassettes of outstanding opera productions, they or any other facsimile will always remain a pale substitute in the estimation of those who truly love the theatre. Nor can even the best of today's sound reproduction equipment for the home fully duplicate the experience of hearing a great orchestra from a good position in a fine auditorium.

The fact that musicians – solo instrumentalists, singers, orchestras and choruses – require regular employment is another strong incentive for maintaining and even expanding concert life. Furthermore, as I am sure Gould would agree, not all those who attend concerts are cellophane crinklers, cultural snobs, intellectual bounders, victims of mass psychosis or plain time-wasters. Some go because they feel that music and musicians deserve their support, while others, amazingly enough, make the effort to be in their seats at eight o'clock because they truly love music and prefer to hear it performed in the type of place for which it was written. I am quite certain that my blood pressure rises just as dangerously as does Gould's when someone sitting near me at a concert noisily opens a sweet wrapper or comments audibly on the proceedings; but if the performance I am attending is a fine one, I am willing to make the sacrifice.

Gould's own successful careers as broadcaster, professional interviewee and musical man of letters are offshoots of his public career as a performing pianist, brief though that career may have been. It is not unfair to say that these later activities would not have been so readily available to him had he not first startled the world by the magnitude of his pianistic talent; for, intelligent and fascinating man though he is, he quite simply is not as capable of overwhelming excellence in any of those other professions as he is (or was) at the first one.

Some of Gould's writings on music are precisely on target. He is, for example, one of the few Canadian musicians who has had the courage to criticize the stranglehold on musical education in English Canada maintained by the graded examination system of Toronto's Royal Conservatory; and he has also written very pointedly about what he calls the

minor-league festival tradition in English Canada – one which is concerned not with the do or die fortunes of budding professionals but with an annual series of regional adjudications for students, presided over by superannuated British academicians. At these events . . . a mark of eighty is automatically accorded a contestant merely for showing up (seventy-nine is considered a stain upon the family honour and reserved for platform indiscretions of a most grievous order. . .).

The adjudicators, moreover, being compelled to deliver their remarks before the assembled parents, neighbours, and schoolmates of the respective contestants, develop an altogether endearing strain of report-card euphemism: 'I say, that's jolly good, Number 67 – smashing spirit and all that. Have to dock you just a point for getting tangled at the double bars, though. Four times through the old exposition is a bit much of a good thing, what?'[10]

But what counts about Gould now, and particularly for this book's purposes, is his recordings. Unfortunately, it is even more difficult to talk about these than about his ideas. They cause in the listener the strangest combination of delight and revulsion that any pianist has ever both been capable of creating and chosen to create – and I know that I am far from being alone in this estimation. There are, for example, his performances of Bach: immediately one thinks of his brilliant and enlivening recordings of the 'Goldberg' Variations, the B-flat major and A minor Partitas, and other works as well; then just as quickly one recalls his callous vivisection of the D major Toccata. Beethoven: the wonderful proportions and grasp of form demonstrated by Gould in the First and Third Piano Concerti are balanced by the preposterous distortion of the first movement of the 'Appassionata' Sonata and the headlong sprint through the first movement of the Sonata Op. 111. Mozart: as if to prove to us that the striking intensity of his performance of the C minor Piano Concerto, K. 491, is not to be taken too seriously, he subjects us to a crazy and bloodless version of the D minor Fantasia, K. 397.

Gould, at his best, is a rhapsodic musician: he pulls the listener naturally and securely into the very heart of the music he is playing. The technique, intelligence and instinct are all extraordinary, all functioning; and there is an ecstatic quality, too – something Gould has frequently referred to in his writings as a *sine qua non* of music-making. But there are other times when that quality is not at all present, when Gould neglects the flow of the music in order to prove that bottom may be called top, if one likes, and east west. The music then becomes a game in which any rules that please the player are acceptable. At this point, the rhapsodic approach is entirely abandoned in favour of a surgical one; the music is dismembered and some bit of it set before us for our edification. As the years go by, Gould seems to be selecting this interpretative method more and more often.

To state the case differently: if one asked most major musicians what the essence of their job consists in, they would probably say something to the effect that they have to try to come to an understanding of all the elements – structural, harmonic, contrapuntal and so on – of a composition, and then to integrate all of those elements in a convincing way. The results each of them will obtain in a given work will probably differ widely from those of his colleagues: and each will probably change his way of playing the piece over a period of years. Nevertheless, the aim is common to most of them. Gould, on the other hand, is not necessarily seeking a well-balanced performance. He may record a piece several times, each time approaching it in a very different way, and then either choose one version or combine two or more by splicing them together. He is by no means telling the listener that this is the way he conceives of a work at this period in his life; he is simply saying that this is one interesting way of looking at this work. The perils of such an approach, intriguing though it may be, are obvious: one may begin to give undue emphasis to certain features of a piece and neglect others, X-ray the tenor line and push the soprano into the background, exaggerate the contrapuntal element in an essentially homophonic piece, and so on. At this point, the procedures of Mr Gould, the musician's pianist, and those of Mr Horowitz, the pianist's pianist, begin, strangely, to converge. '. . . Do something with the music', says Horowitz. 'It may even be something you don't like, but do it!' Is the result of this attitude very different from that of Gould's far more convoluted theorizing? With a pianist like Vladimir Ashkenazy or Maurizio Pollini one

193

is sure, at the very minimum, that the piece of music being performed will have been studied with the aim of presenting it as a unified entity. With a Horowitz or a Gould no such security is possible, for the performer's sense of responsibility to the music and the public has been replaced by his sense of responsibility to his own originality as a performer.

Geoffrey Payzant, a member of the University of Toronto's Philosophy Department, has written a book called *Glenn Gould: Music and Mind*. This book performs several useful services: it sets forth the outlines of Gould's life and career, contains the most important fragments of some of his writings on a variety of subjects, makes use of many people's comments on his work and ideas and includes a Gould discography and other worthwhile information. But the book's earnestness is both exaggerated and out of place. Occasionally, it is reminiscent of the Variorum Shakespeare or the Talmud: a line of Writ is followed by ten of interpretative commentary. Gould's writings, although often clever and sometimes amusing, do not merit this sort of attention. He is a philosopher in the way in which most of us are philosophers: he supplies a philosophy in order to justify his own deeds and predilections. That he achieves this more effectively than most of us are capable of doing may make his rationalizations fun to read, but it does not transform them into anything other than rationalizations.

Quite a few years ago Gould wrote:

In the best of all possible worlds, art would be unnecessary. Its offer of restorative, placative therapy would go begging a patient. The professional specialization involved in its making would be presumption. The generalities of its applicability would be an affront. The audience would be the artist and their life would be art. [11]

Art, however, is a great deal more than a form of therapy – restorative, placatory or otherwise. It stimulates and disturbs far more than it tranquillizes, heightens and sharpens awareness more than it pacifies. Presumably 'the best of all possible worlds', according to Gould, would be one in which every human being would be intellectually capable of living life to the fullest and spiritually capable of coming to terms with himself and everyone around him. But even if such a thing could happen, would every person live life and accept others' lives in the same way? Would all people, in short, be the same person? If not, the need for communication among human beings would be increased rather than decreased; and art is above all a concentrated form of communication. Only a world without death – the one inescapable human truth – could afford to be a world without art. The translation of thought and feeling into complicated symbols is only secondarily a method by which artists isolate and protect themselves. It is much more often, much more powerfully, an impulse to speak out clearly and intensely, to share one's visions, be they heartening or horrifying.

In reality, art is a 'professional specialization' not only because artists are, or ought to be, especially gifted at assimilating, adorning and expressing their experiences, but also because they are generally incapable of doing anything else. They can only face their private heavens and hells by recounting them, passing them down the line. If all people were artists, civilization would quickly grind to a halt.

Payzant ends his book on Gould with an encomium which strikes me not only as overstated, but also as incorrect:

Every Gould recording, like every Gould essay, script, film, documentary and composition, is part of his Promethean effort to share with us the ecstatic awareness of his own many-dimensional, tonal, imaginative perspectives. Gould is the oldtime sage . . . in whom are united the philosopher, the poet and the musician. We diminish him when we confine him to one or another, and we diminish ourselves. [12]

But the point, once again, is that while Gould is a very clever man, and one who is skilled in a number of areas, playing the piano is what he really does best. No one wants him to confine his activities; but what many of us would like him to do is to step out of his antiseptic little corner, move among sweating humanity, and remember that Bach and Beethoven and Schoenberg, like the rest of us but unlike the Moog synthesizer, also lived, loved, perspired and died.

Gould has a wonderful analytical ability; his grasp of the rules of the musical game puts him in a very elite class indeed. That, however, is not enough. The true *magister ludi* does not merely twirl the dials from a glass booth: he stakes his life on every move in the proceedings.

In 1981, twenty-five years after the publication of Gould's 'Goldberg' Variations recording, CBS issued a two-record 'Glenn Gould Silver Jubilee Album'. One of the two discs is occupied entirely by what is billed as 'a Glenn Gould Fantasy, in which Glenn Gould single-handedly takes on a distinguished panel of "musicologists" and "journalists" . . .' It is, of course, essentially Gould interviewing himself, assuming the roles of a sharp-tongued British conductor who considers Gould's ideas and recordings to be so much rubbish, an overly serious German musicologist who agrees with Gould's motives and elucidates his deeds, and others as well. The humour of this record, with its not very convincing foreign accents and its rehashing – yet again – of the Gould Ethic, is at best heavy-handed and at worst junior-high-schoolish. As I sat listening to this latest piece of self-indulgent twaddle (occasionally chuckling, I admit, over some particularly childish nonsense) it occurred to me that a performer is, after all, a performer. Despite all these years of isolation, the man who renounced the concert platform still wants to occupy centre stage, albeit electronically, still wants us to admire and perhaps even to love him, albeit from a safe distance.

One can only sympathize with Gould for the misery he felt during his years on the concert circuit; and I for one admire the courage he demonstrated in ending that part of his career when it was at its height. If his story continues along the lines it has been following, he will end up as a small footnote in the history of musical performance – an exceptional pianist who will leave behind him a few stunning recordings and a much larger body of almost perversely eccentric ones. Because he is a non-competitive man, this prospect presumably does not bother him. It does disturb those of us who consider his to be one of the great pianistic gifts of the century and who wish that he would not withhold from us the grippingly brilliant music-making of which he is capable.

Notes

❖❖❖❖❖❖❖❖❖❖❖❖❖❖❖❖❖❖❖❖❖❖❖❖❖❖❖❖❖❖❖

Introduction

1. Wanda Landowska, *Landowska on Music*, p. 156.
2. Antoine Ysaÿe and Bertram Ratcliff, *Ysaÿe*, p. 31.
3. C. P. E. Bach, *Essay on the True Art of Keyboard Instruments*, p. 152.
4. ibid., p. 1.

Chapter One. Paganini

1. Stendhal, *Vie de Rossini*, p. 451.
2. R. de Saussine, *Paganini*, p. 15.
3. Carl Flesch, *Memoirs*, pp. 2–3.
4. Arturo Codignola, *Paganini intimo*, p. 321.
5. ibid., p. 341.
6. Saussine, op. cit., p. 9.
7. Margaret Campbell, *The Great Violinists*, p. 9.
8. Mario Codignola, *Arte e magia di Niccolò Paganini*, p. 19.
9. ibid., p. 22.
10. Charlotte Moscheles, *Life of Moscheles*, Vol. I, pp. 252–7.
11. G. I. C. de Courcy, *Paganini the Genoese*, Vol. I, pp. 66–7.
12. ibid., pp. 112–13.
13. ibid., p. 125.
14. Berthold Litzmann, *Clara Schumann*, Vol. I, p. 18.
15. Felix Mendelssohn, *Letters to Ignaz and Charlotte Moscheles*, p. 9.
16. Arturo Codignola, op. cit., p. 286.
17. ibid., p. 287.
18. ibid., p. 289.
19. Tibaldi Chiesa, *Paganini*, p. 452.
20. ibid., p. 453.
21. Courcy, op. cit., Vol. II, p. 15.
22. ibid.

23. ibid.
24. Eugène Delacroix, *Journal*, p. 423.
25. Arturo Codignola, op. cit., pp. 332–5.
26. Moscheles, op. cit., Vol. I, pp. 352–7.
27. Arturo Codignola, op. cit., pp. 340–46.
28. ibid., p. 342.
29. Courcy, op. cit., Vol. II, p. 55.
30. Hector Berlioz, *Mémoires*, p. 193.
31. ibid., p. 194.
32. ibid., p. 216.
33. Sir Charles Hallé, *Life and Letters of Sir Charles Hallé*, pp. 62–3.
34. Berlioz, op. cit., p. 219.
35. F.-J. Fétis, *Biographie universelle des musiciens*, Vol. VI, pp. 410–12.
36. Michelangelo Abbado, 'Paganini', in *Rizzoli-Ricordi Enciclopedia della Musica*.
37. Fétis, op. cit., pp. 410–12.
38. Tibaldi Chiesa, op. cit., p. 458.
39. Abbado, op. cit.

Chapter Two. Liszt

1. La Mara (ed.), *Letters of Franz Liszt*, p. 7.
2. Mendelssohn, op. cit., p. 204.
3. Moscheles, op. cit., Vol. I, p. 143.
4. Robert Schumann, *Music and Musicians*, p. 145.
5. Hallé, op. cit., p. 37.
6. Victor Walter, 'Reminiscences of Anton Rubinstein', in *Musical Quarterly*, p. 17.
7. Reginald R. Gerig, *Great Pianists and Their Technique*.
8. Eduard Hanslick, *Vienna's Golden*

Years of Music, pp. 110–13.

9. Alan Walker (ed.), *Frédéric Chopin*, p. 307.
10. Gordon S. Haight (ed.), *The George Eliot Letters*, Vol. II, pp. 169 et seq.; and J. W. Cross (ed.), *George Eliot's Life*, Vol. I, pp. 344 et seq.
11. Alan Walker (ed.), *Franz Liszt*.
12. Hanslick, op. cit., pp. 113–15.
13. Gerig, op. cit., pp. 172–3.
14. Mendelssohn, op. cit., pp. 203–4.
15. ibid.
16. Moscheles, op. cit., Vol. II, p. 87.
17. ibid., p. 203.
18. Litzmann, op. cit., Vol. I, pp. 198 et seq.
19. ibid.
20. ibid., pp. 401, 417.
21. Alan Walker (ed.), *Robert Schumann*, pp. 432–3.
22. Litzmann, op. cit., Vol. I, p. 416.
23. Schumann, op. cit., p. 145.
24. ibid., p. 154.
25. Litzmann, op. cit., Vol. II, p. 121.
26. ibid., p. 263.
27. Hallé, op. cit., pp. 37–9.
28. Hector Berlioz, *Les Soirées de l'orchestre*, p. 420.
29. Camille Saint-Saëns, *Portraits et souvenirs*, pp. 42–3.
30. Amy Fay, *Music-Study in Germany*, pp. 227–8.
31. ibid., pp. 207–9.
32. ibid., p. 220.
33. ibid., p. 223.
34. ibid., pp. 227–8.
35. ibid., pp. 269–70.
36. Gilles Hamelin (ed.), *Emil Sauer*, p. 3.
37. ibid., p. 13.
38. ibid., p. 5.
39. ibid., p. 14.
40. J. A. Fuller-Maitland, *A Door-Keeper of Music*, pp. 116–17.
41. C. F. Weitzmann, *A History of Pianoforte-Playing and Pianoforte-Literature*, pp. 190–91.
42. Gerig, op. cit., pp. 193–4.

Chapter Three. Rubinstein

1. Anton Rubinstein, *Autobiography*.
2. ibid.
3. Oskar von Riesemann, *Rachmaninoff's Recollections*, p. 51.
4. Rubinstein, op. cit.
5. Hanslick, op. cit., p. 264.
6. Rubinstein, op. cit.
7. Anton Rubinstein, *Anton Rubinstein's Gedankenkorb*.
8. Rubinstein, *Autobiography*.
9. ibid.
10. ibid.
11. Litzmann, op. cit., Vol. II, pp. 39–40.
12. Moscheles, op. cit., Vol. II, p. 100.
13. Alexander McArthur, *Anton Rubinstein*, pp. 14–15.
14. Rubinstein, *Autobiography*.
15. ibid.
16. ibid.
17. ibid.
18. Ysaÿe and Ratcliff, op. cit., p. 24.
19. La Mara, op. cit., p. 195.
20. La Mara (ed.), *Briefwechsel zwischen Franz Liszt und Hans von Bülow*, p. 89.
21. La Mara (ed.), *Letters of Franz Liszt*, p. 219.
22. Moscheles, op. cit., Vol. II, p. 251.
23. Saint-Saëns, op. cit., p. 144.
24. Litzmann, op. cit., Vol. III, pp. 19 et seq.
25. ibid.
26. Rubinstein, *Autobiography*.
27. ibid.
28. ibid.
29. Leopold Auer, *My Long Life in Music*, pp. 114–15.
30. Litzmann, op. cit., Vol. III, p. 225.
31. Rubinstein, *Gedankenkorb*.
32. Rubinstein, *Autobiography*.
33. Catherine Drinker Bowen, *Free Artist*, pp. 248–50.
34. Litzmann, op. cit., Vol. III, p. 463.
35. Rubinstein, *Autobiography*.
36. Bowen, op. cit., pp. 317–18.
37. ibid., p. 324.
38. ibid., pp. 354–5.
39. Litzmann, op. cit., Vol. III, p. 590.

40. Hanslick, op. cit., pp. 264–7.
41. Riesemann, op. cit., pp. 51–2.
42. ibid., p. 52.
43. Gerig, op. cit., p. 291.
44. Litzmann, op. cit., Vol. III, p. 225.
45. G. Bernard Shaw, *London Music in 1888–89*.
46. Fuller-Maitland, op. cit., p. 117.
47. James G. Huneker, *Unicorns*, pp. 171–2.
48. Rubinstein, *Autobiography*.
49. Gerig, op. cit., p. 236.
50. ibid., p. 291.
51. McArthur, op. cit., p. 139.
52. ibid., pp. 140–41.
53. Rubinstein, *Autobiography*.
54. Moscheles, op. cit., Vol. II, p. 251.
55. McArthur, op. cit., p. 147.
56. Anton Rubinstein, *Music and its Masters*.

Chapter Four. Paderewski

1. Helena Modjeska, *Memories and Impressions*, pp. 466–8.
2. Alfred Nossig, *I. J. Paderewski*, p. 18.
3. Artur Rubinstein, *My Young Years*, pp. 77–8.
4. Flesch, op. cit., pp. 288–9.
5. Shaw, op. cit., pp. 375–6.
6. Ignace J. Paderewski and Mary Lawton, *The Paderewski Memoirs*.
7. ibid.
8. ibid.
9. Fuller-Maitland, op. cit., p. 199.
10. Shaw, op. cit., pp. 375–6.
11. Paderewski and Lawton, op. cit.
12. Marion Moore Coleman, *Fair Rosalind*, pp. 620–21.
13. ibid.
14. William Mason, 'Paderewski: A Critical Study', *The Century*.
15. Richard Aldrich, *Concert Life in New York, 1902–1923*, pp. 104–5.
16. Paderewski and Lawton, op. cit.
17. ibid.
18. F. W. Gaisberg, *Music on Record*, p. 175.
19. ibid., p. 177.
20. Rom Landau, *Ignace Paderewski*, p. 267.
21. Fuller-Maitland, op. cit., pp. 200–01.
22. Artur Rubinstein, *My Many Years*, pp. 317–18.
23. Artur Schnabel, *My Life and Music*, p. 199.
24. Harriet Cohen, *A Bundle of Time*, p. 106.
25. André Benoist, *The Accompanist . . . and Friends*, pp. 259–60.

Chapter Five. Kreisler

1. Sigmund Freud, *Brautbriefe*.
2. Louis P. Lochner, *Fritz Kreisler*, p. 2.
3. ibid., p. 11.
4. ibid., p. 18.
5. ibid., p. 19.
6. ibid., p. 78.
7. Aldrich, op. cit., pp. 86–7.
8. Benoist, op. cit., p. 231.
9. Aldrich, op. cit., p. 602.
10. Lochner, op. cit., p. 189.
11. Henry T. Finck, *Success in Music, and How it is Won*, pp. 364–5.
12. Flesch, op. cit., p. 118.
13. ibid., p. 121.
14. ibid., pp. 121–2.
15. ibid., p. 122.
16. ibid., p. 125.
17. Lochner, op. cit., pp. 334–5.
18. Benoist, op. cit., pp. 88–9.
19. Flesch, op. cit., pp. 120–21.
20. ibid., p. 118.

Chapter Six. Casals

1. Fuller-Maitland, op. cit., p. 195.
2. Gerig, op. cit., p. 193.
3. J. Cuthbert Hadden, *Modern Musicians*, p. 207.
4. J. M. Corredor, *Conversations with Casals*, pp. 202–3.
5. ibid., p. 199.
6. Juliette Alvin, 'The Logic of Casals's Technique', *The Musical Times*.

7. Flesch, op. cit., pp. 235–6.
8. Hadden, op. cit., p. 207.
9. Pablo Casals and Albert E. Kahn, *Joys and Sorrows*, p. 142.
10. Ysaÿe and Ratcliff, op. cit., p. 115.
11. H. L. Kirk, *Pablo Casals*, pp. 323–4.
12. Cohen, op. cit., p. 129.
13. Bernard Shore, *The Orchestra Speaks*, pp. 66–7.
14. Flesch, op. cit., p. 236.
15. Casals and Kahn, op. cit., p. 167.
16. B. H. Haggin, *Music Observed*.
17. Gaisberg, op. cit., pp. 208–9.
18. ibid., p. 208.
19. Cohen, op. cit., p. 129.
20. Casals and Kahn, op. cit., p. 105.
21. Gaisberg, op. cit., p. 211.
22. Kirk, op. cit., p. 274.
23. Gaisberg, op. cit., p. 209.
24. Casals and Kahn, op. cit., p. 257.
25. Corredor, op. cit., p. 224.
26. ibid., p. 229.
27. Gaisberg, op. cit., p. 212.
28. Kirk, op. cit., p. 498.
29. ibid., pp. 528–9.
30. Casals and Kahn, op. cit., p. 17.

Chapter Seven. Landowska

1. Wanda Landowska, *Landowska on Music*, p. 26.
2. ibid., p. 364.
3. ibid., p. 5.
4. ibid., p. 5.
5. ibid., pp. 5–6.
6. Anton Rubinstein, *Music and its Masters*.
7. Howard Schott, 'Wanda Landowska', in *Early Music*, p. 470.
8. Roland Gelatt, *Music Makers*, p. 268.
9. ibid., p. 279.

10. Wanda Landowska, Notes printed on jacket of record 'Landowska Plays Bach'.
11. Schott, op. cit., pp. 470–71.
12. Landowska, *Landowska on Music*, pp. 365–6.

Chapter Eight. Horowitz

1. Schnabel, op. cit., p. 199.
2. Elyse Mach, *Great Pianists Speak for Themselves*, p. 120.
3. ibid.
4. Gelatt, op. cit., p. 235.
5. Haggin, op. cit., pp. 149 et seq.
6. ibid.
7. Mach, op. cit., p. 116.
8. ibid., pp. 121–2.
9. ibid., pp. 117–18.
10. ibid., p. 49.
11. Schnabel, op. cit., p. 189.
12. Landau, op. cit., p. 283.
13. Mach, op. cit., pp. 37–8.
14. ibid., p. 49.
15. ibid., p. 17.

Chapter Nine. Gould

1. Mach, op. cit., p. 113.
2. Geoffrey Payzant, *Glenn Gould: Music and Mind*, p. 22.
3. ibid., p. 120.
4. ibid., p. 56.
5. ibid.
6. Mach, op. cit., p. 94.
7. Glenn Gould, 'The Prospects of Recording', *High Fidelity*, p. 59.
8. ibid., pp. 59–60.
9. Payzant, op. cit., p. 2.
10. ibid., p. 58.
11. Gould, op. cit., p. 63.
12. Payzant, op. cit., p. 145.

Bibliography

Abbado, Michelangelo.
'Paganini', *Rizzoli-Ricordi Enciclopedia della Musica*, Milan.

Aldrich, Richard. *Concert Life in New York, 1902–1923*. New York: G. P. Putnam's Sons 1941.

Alvin, Juliette. 'The Logic of Casals's Technique', *The Musical Times* (December 1930).

Auer, Leopold. *My Long Life in Music*. New York: F. A. Stokes Co. 1923.

Bach, Carl Philipp Emanuel. *Essay on the True Art of Playing Keyboard Instruments*, ed. W. J. Mitchell. London: Eulenburg 1974.

Benoist, André. *The Accompanist . . . and Friends*, ed. J. A. Maltese. Neptune City, N. J.: Paganiniana Publications 1978.

Berlioz, Hector. *Mémoires*. Paris: Michel Lévy Frères 1870.

Berlioz, Hector. *Les Soirées de l'orchestre*. Paris: Gründ 1968.

Bowen, Catherine Drinker. *Free Artist*. New York: Random House 1939.

Campbell, Margaret. *The Great Violinists*. London: Granada 1980.

Casals, Pablo, and Kahn, Albert E. *Joys and Sorrows*. New York: Simon and Schuster 1970.

Codignola, Arturo. *Paganini intimo*. Genoa: Municipio di Genova 1935.

Codignola, Mario. *Arte e magia di Niccolò Paganini*. Milan: Ricordi 1960.

Cohen, Harriet. *A Bundle of Time*. London: Faber & Faber 1969.

Coleman, Marion Moore. *Fair Rosalind*. Cheshire, Conn.: Cherry Hill Books 1969.

Corredor, J. M. *Conversations with Casals*, tr. A. Mangeot. London: Hutchinson 1956.

Courcy, G. I. C. de. *Paganini the Genoese*. Norman: University of Oklahoma Press 1957.

Cross, J. W. (ed.). *George Eliot's Life*. Edinburgh and London: William Blackwood and Sons 1885.

Delacroix, Eugène. *Journal*. Paris: Librairie Plon 1933.

Fay, Amy. *Music-Study in Germany*. Chicago: Jansen, McClurg & Co. 1881.

Fétis, F.-J. *Biographie universelle des musiciens*, IIe édition. Paris: Librairie de Firmin-Didot et C.ie 1878.

Finck, Henry T. *Success in Music, and How it is Won*. London: John Murray 1910.

Flesch, Carl. *Memoirs*, tr. H. Keller. London: Rockliff 1957.

Freud, Sigmund (ed. E. L. Freud). *Brautbriefe*. Hamburg: Fischer 1968.

Fuller-Maitland, J. A. *A Door-Keeper of Music*. London: John Murray 1929.

Gaisberg, F. W. *Music on Record*. London: Robert Hale Ltd. 1946.

Gelatt, Roland. *Music Makers*. New York: Alfred A. Knopf 1953.

Geminiani, Francesco. *A Treatise of Good Taste in the Art of Music*. London: 1749.

Gerig, Reginald R. *Great Pianists and Their Technique*. Newton Abbot. David & Charles 1976.

Gould, Glenn. 'The Prospects of Recording', *High Fidelity Magazine* (April 1966).

Hadden, J. Cuthbert. *Modern*

Musicians. London: Peter Davies Ltd. 1913.

Haggin, B. H. *Music Observed*. New York: Oxford University Press 1964.

Haight, Gordon S. (ed.). *The George Eliot Letters*. New Haven: Yale University Press 1954–5.

Hallé, Sir Charles. *Life and Letters of Sir Charles Hallé*. London: Smith, Elder & Co. 1896.

Hamelin, Gilles (ed.). *Emil Sauer: Disciple of Liszt*. New York: Musical Scope Publishers 1975.

Hanslick, Eduard. *Vienna's Golden Years of Music*, ed. H. Pleasants. London: V. Gollancz 1951.

Huneker, James G. *Unicorns*. London: T. Werner Laurie Ltd. 1918.

Kirk, H. L. *Pablo Casals*. London: Hutchinson & Co. 1974.

La Mara (ed.). *Briefwechsel zwischen Franz Liszt und Hans von Bülow*. Leipzig: Breitkopf & Härtel 1898.

La Mara (ed.). *Letters of Franz Liszt*, tr. C. Bache. London: H. Grevel & Co. 1894.

Landau, Rom. *Ignace Paderewski*. New York: Thomas Y. Crowell 1934.

Landowska, Wanda. *Landowska on Music*, ed. D. Restout and R. Hawkins. London: Secker & Warburg 1965.

Landowska, Wanda. Notes printed on jacket of RCA record VIC-1594, 'Landowska Plays Bach', USA (1971).

Liszt, Franz. *Franz Liszt's Briefe*, ed. La Mara. Leipzig: Breitkopf & Härtel 1893–1905.

Litzmann, Berthold. *Clara Schumann*. Leipzig: Breitkopf & Härtel 1906.

Lochner, Louis P. *Fritz Kreisler*. London: Rockliff 1951.

Mach, Elyse. *Great Pianists Speak for Themselves*. New York: Dodd, Mead & Co. 1980.

Mason, William. 'Paderewski: A Critical Study', *The Century*. New York (March 1892).

McArthur, Alexander (pseud. of McArthur, Lillian). *Anton Rubinstein*. Edinburgh: Adam and Charles Black 1889.

Mendelssohn, Felix. *Letters to Ignaz and Charlotte Moscheles*, ed. F. Moscheles. London: Trübner & Co. 1888.

Modjeska, Helena. *Memories and Impressions*. New York: MacMillan 1910.

Moscheles, Charlotte. *Life of Moscheles*, tr. A. D. Coleridge. London: Hurst & Blackett 1873.

Nossig, Alfred. *I. J. Paderewski*. Leipzig: Hermann Seemann Nachfolger 1901.

Paderewski, Ignace Jan, and Lawton, Mary. *The Paderewski Memoirs*. London: Collins 1939.

Payzant, Geoffrey. *Glenn Gould: Music and Mind*. Toronto: Van Nostrand Reinhold Ltd. 1978.

Plaskin, Glenn. 'The Secret Career of Horowitz', *The New York Times Magazine* (11 May 1980).

Riesemann, Oskar von. *Rachmaninoff's Recollections*. London: George Allen & Unwin Ltd. 1934.

Rubinstein, Anton. *Autobiography*, tr. A. Delano. Boston: Little, Brown & Co. 1890.

Rubinstein, Anton. *Anton Rubinstein's Gedankenkorb*. Leipzig: Verlag von Bartholf Senff 1897.

Rubinstein, Anton. *Music and its Masters*, tr. Mrs. J. P. Morgan. London: Augener Ltd. (1920?)

Rubinstein, Artur. *My Young Years*. London: Jonathan Cape 1973.

Rubinstein, Artur. *My Many Years*. London: Jonathan Cape 1980.

Saint-Saëns, Camille. *Portraits et souvenirs*. Paris: Calmann-Lévy 1909.

Saussine, R. de. *Paganini*. Milan: Nuova Accademia 1958.

Schnabel, Artur. *My Life and Music*. Gerrards Cross: Colin Smythe 1970.

Schott, Howard. 'Wanda Landowska', *Early Music*, VII (1979).

Schumann, Robert. *Music and Musicians*, tr. F. R. Ritter. London: William Reeves 1877.

Shaw, George Bernard. *London Music in 1888–89 as Heard by Corno di Bassetto (Later Known as Bernard Shaw) with Some Further Autobiographical Particulars*. London: Constable & Co. Ltd. 1937.

Shore, Bernard. *The Orchestra Speaks*. London: Longmans, Green & Co. 1938.

Stendhal (Henri Beyle). *Vie de Rossini*. Paris: 1824.

Tibaldi Chiesa, Maria. *Paganini*. Milan: Garzanti 1944.

Walker, Alan (ed.). *Franz Liszt: The Man and His Music*. London: Barrie & Jenkins 1970.

Walker, Alan (ed.). *Frédéric Chopin: The Man and His Music*. London: Barrie & Jenkins 1966.

Walker, Alan (ed.). *Robert Schumann: The Man and His Music*. London: Barrie & Jenkins 1972.

Walter, Victor. 'Reminiscences of Anton Rubinstein', tr. D. A. Modell, *Musical Quarterly*, Vol. V, Pt. II, No. 4 (1919).

Weitzmann, C. F. *A History of Pianoforte-Playing and Pianoforte-Literature*, ed. T. Baker. New York: G. Schirmer 1897.

Ysaÿe, Antoine, and Ratcliff, Bertram. *Ysaÿe*. London: Heinemann 1947.

Index

❖❖

205